Essential
Paris

by

SUSAN GROSSMAN

Susan Grossman is a travel writer, broadcaster, and photographer, and is a former travel editor of the *London Sunday Telegraph Magazine*. She has presented two series of the BBC's 'Food and Drink' program.

D0448443

Little, Brown and Company
Boston   Toronto   London

REVISED EDITION

The contents of this publication are believed correct at the time of printing.
Nevertheless, the publishers cannot accept responsibility for errors or
omissions, nor for changes in details given. We are always grateful to readers
who let us know of any errors or omissions they come across, and future
printings will be updated accordingly.

Produced by the Publishing Division of The Automobile Association of Great
Britain.

Written by Susan Grossman
"Peace and Quiet" Section by Paul Sterry
Consultant: Frank Dawes

The Automobile Association would like to thank the following photographers and libraries
for their assistance in the compilation of the book.

SUSAN GROSSMAN 18 Brasserie Lipp, 22/3 Musée d'Orsay, 25 Picasso Museum, 29 Musée
Rodin, 68 Jo Goldenberg's restaurant, 70/1 Pâtisserie, 72 Café de Flore, 74 Fanny's Tea
Shop, 79 Breakfast Crillon Hotel, 80 Crillon Hotel, 82/3 Henry IV Hotel, 96 Kenzo's Boutique,
102 Le Trumilou, 109 Bus, 121 La Madeleine Church

LANCASTER HOTEL 81 Lancaster Hotel

MARY EVANS PICTURE LIBRARY 9 Siege of the Bastille

NATURE PHOTOGRAPHERS LTD 48 Beechwoods (B Burbidge), 49 Crested Tit (M Gore),
50/1 Common Violet (P Sterry), 53 Red Deer Stag (W S Paton)

BARRIE SMITH 4 Eiffel Tower, 8 Liberty, 11 The Left Bank, 13 Paris Mime, 14/5 Place de la
Concorde, 17 SNCF Train, 20 La Coupole, 21 the Louvre, 26 La Géode, 27 Musée d'Art
Moderne, 30 Arc de Triomphe, 32/3 Notre-Dame Cathedral, 37 Parc de Bagatelle, 46/7 Bois
de Boulogne, 55 Les Halles Forum, 56/7 Galeries Lafayette, 60 Place de la Madeleine, 73
Animal Market, 65 Place St-Michel, 67 Terminus Nord Brasserie, 75 Cheese Shop, 77 & 78
Labels, 88 Seine by Night, 94 Paris Marathon, 95 Place St Jacques, 97 Boy & Camera, 98/9
Musée d'Orsay, 100 Tuileries Gardens, 103 Arc de Triomphe, 104 Traffic, 107 Lunch on
Board, 114/5 Métro, 117 Eiffel Tower, 119 Musée d'Orsay, 122 Seine

SPECTRUM COLOUR LIBRARY 40/1 Parc Monceau, 42 Fontainebleau, 76 Cheese Stall, 78
Wine Tasting

ZEFA PICTURE LIBRARY UK LTD 5 Pompidou Centre, 6/7 Place du Tertre, 24 Sacré Cœur,
44 Versailles, 85 Bâteau mouches, 86 Moulin Rouge, 91 Lido, 92 Pigalle

Author's Acknowledgements
Susan Grossman wishes to thank the luxury Crillon Hotel, 10 place de la Concorde, 8e;
Tradotels, a group of hotels in traditional buildings renovated to 3-star standards; Brymon
Airways, who fly from London City Airport to Paris, and the French Government Tourist
Office for all the help they gave in compiling this book.

ISBN 0-316-25029-5

10 9 8 7 6 5 4 3 2 1

PRINTED IN TRENTO, ITALY

This book employs a
simple rating system to
help choose which
places to visit:

◆◆◆ do not miss

◆◆   see if you can

◆   worth seeing if
    you have time

The Eiffel Tower is Paris's best known monument, though less popular these days than the Beaubourg. At 1,007ft (307m), it was the tallest building in the world when it was constructed in 1889. Made of a latticework of pig iron, it has three platforms and 1,710 steps to the top, though the weary can take an elevator. On a clear day you can see for 45 miles (72km)

INTRODUCTION

Paris is still one of the most romantic, chic and culturally rewarding cities in the world. Nowhere in the world is there such a concentration of quality. You can drool over the exquisite displays of food, chocolates and fashion in the shop windows, and over menus outside restaurants perpetually full of a nation who take eating out almost as seriously as anything clsc and while you *can* spend the earth on anything from an *haute couture* costume to a gourmet meal, Paris can be a remarkably good value.

The city is quite small and most of the main sites are within walking distance of each other. You cannot miss the main landmarks: the Eiffel Tower, the Arc de Triomphe and the Notre-Dame Cathedral, the Beaubourg, the Louvre, and the new Musée d'Orsay. But if you are planning a long weekend it might be an idea to make Friday rather than Monday the additional day, as many museums and some shops shut at the beginning of the week. It is also worth remembering that many museums are free or cheaper on Sunday.

As for *gay Paris,* unlike many other cities, Paris does not close down at midnight. Brasseries stay open until the early hours, and you can dance, visit a cabaret or listen to jazz in a smokey basement until the garbage trucks shatter the silence of the early morning streets.

New Paris

If you have not been to Paris for a while you will find quite a few changes, many of them thanks to an enormous injection of money from President Mitterand to build new monuments and transform old ones. He is not, of course, the first President of France to want to leave his mark on the face of Paris. De Gaulle was responsible for the modern skyline of La Défense to the west of Paris and Pompidou for Paris's number one tourist attraction, the Beaubourg, that bears his name. In the mid-1970s the 59-storey Montparnasse Tower on the Left Bank sprang up. Next came the exodus of Les Halles market, and the redevelopment of the whole site with the underground Forum des Halles shopping centre and the Georges Pompidou Centre of Modern Art.

The controversial Georges Pompidou Centre, or Beaubourg, houses the National Museum of Modern Art, as well as changing exhibitions. Designed by Richard Rogers its 'inside out' appearance has offended many although it certainly pulls in the crowds. Take the escalator up the outside for splendid views of the capital or take advantage of the free shows in the piazza outside

The place du Tertre in Montmartre is where to go to get your portrait etched or sketched – for a price. The highest point in the capital, at 425ft (130m), Montmartre is topped by the icing sugar dome of the Sacré Cœur Cathedral from which there are splendid views, especially at night

In the last few years another major museum, the Cité des Sciences et de l'Industrie, has opened on the site of the slaughterhouses at La Villette in the northeast of Paris, some fifteen minutes by Métro from the centre. Refrigerated trucks had rendered the abbatoirs obsolete, so the whole area has been turned into a *parc* (still to be completed) and science museum designed to help young people 'discover' for themselves through an impressive range of computers, machinery and hands-on exhibits. The complex, which also includes an enormous mirrored dome, La Géode, containing a revolutionary 180-degree cinema, already ranks as one of the capital's major attractions even if the majority of instructions to everything are in French only!

The Louvre is also undergoing change on a large scale. By 1992 it will be the largest museum in the world. The new glass pyramid designed by I.M. Pei at the entrance is already open. The Ministry of Finance that is at present based there will move out to Bercy and underground excavations will create new space for major exhibits.

Paris's collection of Impressionist paintings has been removed from the Jeu de Paume and

other galleries and now sits in splendour on the top floor of the Musée d'Orsay on the Left Bank, the former Gare d'Orsay railway station converted into a magnificent national art gallery.

Other new landmarks include a surrealist 350ft (107m) high marble Arch at La Défense (offices, with an elevator to the top to admire the view), and the modern Institut du Monde Arabe which is already open on the Left Bank, its windows made up of lenses which open and shut with the light.

Chirac's huge Palais Omnisport centre for concerts and sporting events is at Bercy and Disneyland is due to arrive in the early 1990s in Marne La Vallée, the new town in the suburbs. Several areas of Paris have undergone a marked transformation, the Marais and the Bastille on the Right Bank in particular. The new Opera house for the 'people', at the Bastille, is responsible for the changes there and was inaugurated on 13 July 1989, appropriately enough the eve of Bastille Day. The old Opéra, Opéra de Paris – Garnier, is now only used for ballet.

Many of the once derelict *hôtels* (mansions) of the Marais have been smartened up to house offices, restaurants, shops and the new Picasso Museum. Even the historic place des Vosges has been re-landscaped. Over recent years both these areas have taken on some of the character of the *sixième arrondissement* (sixth district), with art galleries, designer showrooms, jazz clubs and restaurants effectively extending the 'arty' side of Paris over the Seine onto the Right Bank.

Like any city, Paris has its down side. There are neons and a McDonald's on the Champs-Elysées, the Latin Quarter is packed with ethnic take-out restaurants and a seedy nightlife prevails in Pigalle, behind the Beaubourg, and near Montparnasse.

Old Paris

But what of the old Paris? You needn't worry. Lovers still walk arm in arm in the Luxembourg gardens and along the Seine. The glass-topped boats chug up and down the river, you can climb the Eiffel Tower, or have your portrait sketched in Montmartre's place du Tertre. The girls at the Folies Bergère and the Lido can-can the night away, while outside the traffic jams up the Champs-Elysées, and races round the place de la Concorde and the Arc de Triomphe as though every driver was on his way to Le Mans. As for the women, young and old, Left Bank or Right, they are still the most elegant in the world.

History
Paris is dominated by the Seine which curves through the centre. Along its banks you will find Paris's most splendid architecture: Notre-Dame Cathedral and the Sainte-Chapelle on the Ile de la Cité, where Paris began, as well as the magnificent Louvre Museum and the Eiffel Tower, the symbol of France itself. The city has had a chequered and bloody history, passing from hand to hand over the centuries.
In the 3rd century BC a Gallic tribe made the Ile de la Cité their fortified capital. In 52 BC Caesar's Roman legions called it Lutetia and turned it into an important Roman centre, its name being changed to Paris in AD 360.

Most of Paris's monuments – old and new – are visible from the Seine

In the Early Middle Ages after the Romans had left, several invasions threatened the civilisation of the city – one by Attila the Hun, though it did not succeed, another by the Franks. During the famine that followed a young woman called Geneviève helped the people and became the patron saint of Paris.
The city was continuously in difficulty with the Norman sieges, and the Hundred Years' War stunted any real development until the time of the Capetien monarchs. Then came the building of Notre-Dame in 1108, the building of

Anon. Revolution. Trouble began on the morning of 14 July 1789 when a militant mob advanced on Les Invalides looking for weapons. They helped themselves to 28,000 rifles and headed for the Bastille where in a symbolic gesture, depicted above, they released all seven prisoners they found there. Bastille Day is celebrated every year with military bands and fireworks

the fortress of the Louvre in 1180 and the establishment of the Sorbonne university in 1285.

Through the reigns of François I, Catherine de'Medici, and Henri III Paris grew, though there were bloody conflicts between Catholics and Protestants. But it was not until the 17th century, and in particular the reign of the Sun King Louis XIV, that Paris really blossomed. Versailles became his Royal Court and Les Invalides, Gobelins, the Louvre colonnade and the Comédie-Française were built. He abolished the municipality and Paris became ruled by the State. By Louis XV's reign the crown was growing steadily more unpopular, there were disastrous overseas wars and financial problems at home although more buildings, the Panthéon, the Palais-Bourbon and the place de la Concorde were completed. Then came the Revolution that changed everything.

On 14 July 1789 (Paris celebrated its bi-centenary in 1989) an angry mob stormed the Bastille and symbolically freed the prisoners and France from the aristocratic State. The following year Louis XVI and his queen, Marie Antoinette, were imprisoned and executed. A Reign of Terror followed where 2,800 people in Paris lost their heads, ending with Napoleon

appointing himself the new dictator in 1799.
From then on Paris became prosperous even
though the city was terrorised by Napoleon. But
in 1814 Paris fell to the invading allied armies
and Napoleon was exiled and fought his last
battle at Waterloo. During the Restoration in the
1840s, the Thiers fortifications were built around
the city, forming the boundary of the present
périphérique (ring road).

Much of the city had been destroyed by the
Revolution. In the 19th century Haussmann
created wide boulevards, dividing up the city
into the present 20 *arrondissements* (districts).
A period of prosperity began in 1870. The Eiffel
Tower was built for the World Exhibition in
1889 (1989 being its centenary), in 1900 the first
Métro line opened and then followed the Belle
Epoque: the days of Maxims, the Folies and the
talents of Picasso, Hemingway, Monet and
Renoir. The city has never looked back.

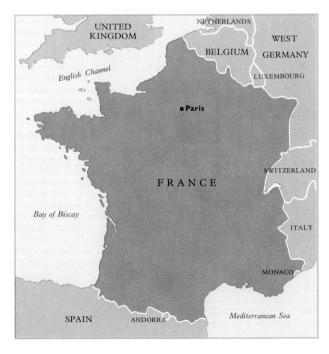

THE DIFFERENT AREAS

Paris is divided up into 20 different numbered areas or *arrondissements* thanks to Baron Haussmann who sliced up the city into neat sections to please Napoleon III. The numbers start at the centre of the city and work outwards in a clockwise spiral. As a general rule once you start getting into double figures you will need to use the Métro to get around.
Each area has its own distinctive character, from the sleazy red light district in the 9e to the wide boulevards and luxury hotels in the neighbouring 8e (*er* or *e* is the abbreviation used for *premier, deuxième*, etc *arrondissement*). Although the boundaries are clearly defined officially, some areas described by name, like the Marais, spill over into more than one numbered area. Your first decision is whether to stay on the Right or the Left Bank of the River Seine.

THE RIGHT BANK

The Right Bank is, on the whole,

The quais *along the Seine are lined with* bouquinistes *plying their trade with second-hand books, postcards and prints*

grander than the Left. It is where the main monuments are, the large department stores, the *haute couture* boutiques, the Louvre, the Beaubourg, the Tuileries, the Opéra, the Champs-Elysées, the Bastille and the Marais as well as the red light district of Pigalle, and gay (literally) Paris around Les Halles.

THE LEFT BANK

The Left is more Bohemian in parts but no less chic. It is called the Latin Quarter, and is largely inhabited by students and the ethnic population of the city. It includes the Eiffel Tower, the Luxembourg Gardens, St-Germain-des-Prés, the Musée d'Orsay with its magnificent collection of Impressionist paintings, numerous boutiques, art galleries, late night bars, cafés, jazz clubs, street markets and restaurants of every nationality.

THE DIFFERENT AREAS

But Paris is small — all you have to do to get from one side to the other is stroll over one of the many bridges.

If you are unfamiliar with the city you may like to know a bit about the character of each *arrondissement* and the different areas. If you want a central hotel choose one in the following areas (in a rough rank order of preference): 6e, 1er, 8e, 2e, 4e, 5e, 7e, 3e, 9e, 10e, 14e and forget about the rest unless you do not mind driving or taking public transportation into the centre.

For more about what to see within each area, see What to See, pages 21-44.

The Right Bank

LOUVRE, PALAIS ROYAL (1er and 2e)
The centre of Paris, the Right Bank of the River Seine. Home of many of the large luxury hotels, the sort you arrive at by taxi rather than on foot. The area also includes the Louvre, the Conciergerie on the IIe de la Cité, the grand avenue leading up to the Opéra (which has airlines and tourist offices), an assortment of shops including fashionable boutiques and exclusive jewellers in and around the place Vendôme and to a lesser extent in the rue de Rivoli, the trendy boutiques in the place des Victoires, the antique shops opposite the Louvre, the Tuileries Gardens, many offices, and major institutions, the Bourse, the Bibliothèque National, and the

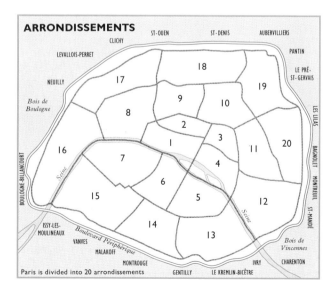

Paris is divided into 20 arrondissements

arcaded 19th-century *passages* around the Palais Royal.

FORUM DES HALLES/ BEAUBOURG (part of the 1er, 4e, and part of 3e)

Touristy is the best way to describe this area. Still undecided as to its true identity, it is a mix of modern glass and chrome covering the largest underground shopping area in Europe, the Forum des Halles, and somewhat sleazy side streets around it with neons, cafés, and sex shops in the rue St-Denis and bars and jazz clubs towards Châtelet. Les Halles was Paris's main market, moving out after 800 years in 1969 and leaving a vast hole that was eventually filled by the shopping centre and neighbouring Beaubourg, the name given to the controversial inside-out Georges Pompidou Centre, the National Museum of Modern Art. Opened in 1977 and now more popular than the Eiffel Tower, you can travel up the outside on an escalator from where there are splendid views of Notre-Dame, the Eiffel Tower and other major sites. The whole area is a mecca for visitors. The piazza in front of it is always packed with people watching the free street shows: jugglers, musicians, portrait painters and others entertaining the crowds. You can sit down and watch in one of the (expensive) cafés, if you can find a seat. It is not difficult to distinguish the Parisian offspring in their designer clothes from overseas children in grubby jeans and T-shirts. Central to stay in, but crowded.

The biggest free show in Paris takes place in the piazza outside the Beaubourg

LES ILES (ST LOUIS, DE LA CITÉ) (4e, 1er)

Still on the Right Bank, but peaceful and relatively calm after the bustle of the main boulevards — though nevertheless pretty crowded, especially on warm afternoons. Two tiny islands in the Seine, where Paris began, right in the heart of the city and dominated by Notre-Dame Cathedral, the Palais de Justice, the Sainte-Chapelle and the Conciergerie. An area of shady squares and Seine views. The few hotels that are there are much sought after and difficult to get into.

THE DIFFERENT AREAS

The **Ile St Louis** is the quieter of the two islands with narrow streets — the main one running across the centre — and tall 17th-century houses. Named after a French king who came to meditate when it was just a cow pasture, it was settled in the early 17th century. You can relax on the *quais* (there is a tree-lined walk) or have a drink or a snack in one of the bars or outdoor cafés or a cone full of the best ice-cream in Paris from Berthillon's.

The **Ile de la Cité** is approached by the Pont Neuf, the city's oldest bridge. This is where it all began, on a natural defence in the river, settled by the Romans. On the Ile de la Cité you will find the quiet place Dauphine, the Sainte-Chapelle with its splendid stained-glass windows and the Conciergerie where Marie Antoinette was imprisoned. There is a flower market in the place Louis-Lépine, with birds for sale on Sundays, and, of course, the magnificent Gothic Notre-Dame Cathedral. If you stand outside the Cathedral's west door there is a spot on the pavement known as *kilomètre zéro* from which all distances in France are marked.

THE MARAIS, RÉPUBLIQUE (3e, 4e)

The Marais, on the Right Bank between the Beaubourg and the Bastille, is the oldest, and one of the most interesting, areas of Paris. It is relatively calm, quiet and devoid of traffic compared to other parts of Paris. Once inhabited by the aristocracy, its fortunes changed with the Revolution when its proximity to the Bastille and its prison turned the elegant Marais into the all too familiar setting of Victor Hugo's *Les Misérables*.

Although recently renovated it has been spared the bulldozers and most of the 17th-century mansions or *hôtels* as they are called have been carefully converted into offices, boutiques, apartments and museums, including the magnificent Picasso Museum in the Hôtel Salé, the Hôtel Carnavalet in the rue de Sévigné (which holds major exhibitions from time to time), and the Museum Victor Hugo in the place des Vosges, Paris's most beautiful square with *hôtels*, interesting shops and several good restaurants beneath the arcades.

The place de la Concorde

Property prices have escalated and rooms once inhabited by the hungry poor are now filled with the hungry rich who are sitting on a potential gold mine, sure to explode with the opening of the new Opera House for the 'people'. Designer boutiques, ultra modern furniture showrooms and art galleries open by the day, but the area is still full of the old craftsmen. This is where to come if you want a picture framed or a handbag repaired. It is also the centre of the rag trade, and the home of the Jewish community, with synagogues and delis and middle European restaurants (some Russian) concentrated between the rue des Ecouffes and rue des Rosiers.

Paris's gay community congregates in bars and discreet clubs along the rue Ste-Croix-de-la-Bretonnerie. But

it is all very low key and stylish. There are also clubs and discos in the quartier du Temple just south of the République and just north of the Hôtel-de-Ville.

The hotels in this area get cheaper as you get towards the République; some are in converted mansions near the place des Vosges.

CHAMPS-ELYSÉES, MADELEINE and PLACE DE LA CONCORDE (8e)

A big bustling area with expensive hotels around the Champs-Elysées, exclusive fashion salons in the avenue Montaigne and rue du Faubourg-St-Honoré and fabulous food shops (Fauchon, Hédiard) in the place de la Madeleine, with high-class tarts behind it in the rue de Sèze.

The famous Champs-Elysées stretches for 1.1 miles (1.8 km) from the Arc de Triomphe to the place de la Concorde, often one long traffic jam, lined with neon-lit cinemas, airline offices, banks, bars, and overpriced restaurants and cafés. You will also find the Lido cabaret, and hordes of weekend revellers who get off the RER express train at Etoile and hang around the Drugstore and the fast-food outlets like McDonald's and Burger King. One of its famous landmarks, Fouquets, where De Gaulle and Churchill used to lunch, narrowly escaped being turned into a hamburger bar by its Kuwaiti owners. The Government, horrified at the prospect, intervened and declared it a national historic monument.

THE DIFFERENT AREAS

In the place de la Concorde you will see the obelisk from the Temple of Luxor in Egypt and the grand de Crillon hotel, the only luxury hotel left still owned by the French.

This area does not have to be prohibitively expensive. The department stores are only just over the boundary into the 9e, the quieter residential area near the parc Monceau has medium priced hotels and good restaurants, and prices drop considerably towards the Gare St-Lazare which is still within walking distance of the centre.

OPÉRA, DEPARTMENT STORES and PIGALLE (9e)

The area with the largest number of hotels and probably the most mixed in character. It stretches from the busy boulevard Haussmann with the enormous department stores (Galeries Lafayette, Printemps, Monoprix and M&S), to the Paris Opéra, past major banks to the Folies Bergère and the sleazy low life of Clichy and Pigalle — the red light district with its strip clubs and sex shows. You should avoid staying in the northern part of this *arrondissement* if you possibly can, even though numerous tour operators will try to persuade you otherwise. (See Paris by Night, pages 85-92)

GARE DU NORD and GARE DE L'EST (10e)

Cheap, busy and generally a bit drab and depressing. This is where you will arrive if you come in by train from the airport. Your hotel may be noisy but it will cost a lot less than in other areas of Paris and if you

are only looking for somewhere to put your head down, and do not intend to spend much time in it, you are not too far from the centre. Nothing much of interest to see.

BASTILLE (11e, 12e)

The Bastille (11e and 12e), home of the famous prison stormed by angry mobs on 14 July 1789, is now *the* up-and-coming area of Paris. The new Opera House for the people nearby, which looks much like an office block, was inaugurated on 13 July 1989. The area is still mixed in character — alongside the modern art galleries, trendy nightclubs, brasseries, cafés and retro-fashion boutiques there are cheap furniture shops, a fairground and dingy bars. Nightlife concentrates itself in a triangle between the rue de Lappe, rue de Charonne and rue de la Roquette and includes an old music hall of the 1930s where old timers still dance Saturday afternoons away and the *branché* young line up for rock bands in the evenings. The neighbouring 12e is a suburb some way from the centre. It includes the Gare de Lyon and the vast Palais d'Omnisports de Bercy which offers large audiences anything from rock concerts to ice hockey matches. The Seine is lined with old warehouses that are being slowly bought up by developers. Thousands of boats are moored on the western edge of the 12e in the Paris Arsenal. You can take a barge north up to La Villette (see pages 24-26) (under the Bastille) or to explore the canals. The 12e

ends at the *périphérique* on the edge of the Bois de Vincennes which has a zoo and a small boating lake (see Parks and Gardens, page 36).

THE 16e and 17e

The 16e, near the Bois de Boulogne, is where the most wealthy Parisians have their apartments. It is very chic, very fashionable and very expensive. There is little of interest for visitors apart from the shops in the avenue Victor Hugo and avenue Foch, some of the best restaurants, the Palais de Chaillot, and the Palais de Tokyo (devoted to photography), and an impressive collection of Monet paintings in the Musée Marmottan. The village areas of Auteuil and Passy have more character, with fashionable boutiques in the rue de Passy. There are some elegant,

High speed trains dispatch visitors at the Gare du Nord

old-fashioned hotels in the area if you do not mind being some way from the centre.

There are also comfortable hotels in the residential, though less exclusive, 17e and some huge modern luxury hotels catering to businessmen around the busy Porte Maillot and Palais des Congrès convention centre.

MONTMARTRE (18e)

The old artists' quarter topped by the icing sugar dome of Sacré-Cœur Cathedral, sadly overrun by visitors having their portraits etched and sketched in the place du Tertre at the top of the hill. You can get a funicular up or walk on the quiet southwest side up the rue Lepic. Once at the top there are a number of (over-priced) open-air cafés, with

THE DIFFERENT AREAS

The Brasserie Lipp, in the Latin Quarter on the Left Bank in St-Germain, is where to watch Parisians go by. One-time haunt of Sartre

accompanying accordionists and wonderful views across Paris from the Cathedral. To the east is the Marché Saint-Pierre, which sells colourful fabrics. There are ethnic shops in the surrounding streets. Property is cheap and there are plenty of reasonably priced hotels. The sleazy boulevard Clichy and boulevard Pigalle are at the bottom of the hill. To the north of Montmartre is the flea market at the Porte de Clignancourt.

THE 19e and 20e

The northeast of Paris. In the 19e is the site of the new parc de Villette and its various attractions including the Cité des Sciences et de l'Industrie and the Buttes de Chaumont park. You would not want to stay so far out and there are few hotels.

The 20e is even less inspiring. It includes the Père Lachaise cemetery and the weekend and Monday flea market for secondhand clothes at the Porte de Montreuil.

The Left Bank

THE LATIN QUARTER (5e, 6e)

For first-time visitors the Left Bank's Latin Quarter somehow feels more Parisian. It's livelier, the streets are narrower, the boutiques less formidable, the famous cafés in the boulevard St-Germain more crowded. The place St-Michel is the centre of the Latin Quarter proper, the 5e. The place St-Germain is the centre of the 6e, which is on the whole more expensive and more elegant than the student-land of the 5e.

The 5e includes the Panthéon, the Sorbonne university, the student and ethnic population of the city, the Jardin des Plantes, and one of the best food markets, in the rue Mouffetard. There are plenty of reasonably priced hotels and restaurants of every nationality, including numerous Greek and North African restaurants in the pedestrian-only rue Huchette, which also offers one of the few authentic jazz clubs, Les Caves de Huchette.

The new Institut du Monde Arabe in the quai Saint-Bernard, with its windows made up of giant lenses that open and shut with the sun, is also in the 5e. All in all, an area that appeals to those on a budget.

ST-GERMAIN (6e)

Centre of the arts and fashion world. Not *haute couture* but designer chic. A relatively small area on the other side of the Seine from the Louvre, centred around St-Germain-des-Prés and extending south to the Luxembourg gardens. St-Germain-des-Prés gained its reputation after the war when its inexpensive restaurants and bars became the meeting place for intellectuals and artists. The cafés (Flore, Lipp and Deux Magots) frequented by Jean Paul Sartre and Simone de Beauvoir are still there and everyone still watches the world go by, but the prices can be prohibitively expensive. There are numerous boutiques.

To the north of the boulevard St-Germain the narrow streets are full of small hotels, art galleries, bookshops, antique shops, elegant boutiques, and restaurants. The best streets for shopping are rue Jacob and the rue Bonaparte and, south of St-Germain, the place St-Sulpice and the Cherche-Midi. There is also a lively food market that takes up most of the rue de Buci and rue de Seine.

There are numerous hotels, some with pretty courtyards, many old 17th- and 18th-century houses with a steep climb up to the fifth-floor rooms. You will be a stone's throw from the Seine and the bridges across to the Right Bank. If you can find a hotel room in this area you should take it.

INVALIDES, MUSÉE D'ORSAY and THE EIFFEL TOWER (7e)

Quiet, staid and a bit lacking in atmosphere compared to other parts of Paris. But still very central. The buildings are magnificent 17th-, 18th- and 19th-century private residences, many of them ministries and embassies and the broad tree-lined streets are generally quiet unless you happen to be around when one or other section of the population is demonstrating about something. There are usually police in front of the high-walled private house of the Prime Minister and outside the Foreign Office.

To cater to the embassies and ministers, the 7e has a large number of Paris's best restaurants and some up-market designer boutiques in the rue de Grenelle and rue St-Dominique as well as the Au Bon Marché department store. The main sites are the Eiffel Tower, the new Musée d'Orsay in the old railway station, with its national art collection including Impressionist paintings, and the Rodin Museum.

Few visitors stay in this area of Paris, although there are numerous quiet hotels and it is easy to walk both to the Latin Quarter (6e) and across to the Louvre and Right Bank.

MONTPARNASSE (14e, 15e)

Both areas are huge, but provided you are staying in the north of either *arrondissement*, near to Montparnasse, you will not be too far from the centre. The steel and smoked-glass, 59-storey Tour Montparnasse was completed in the mid-1970s

— somewhat of an eyesore, but there are splendid views of Paris from the top, and a large shopping complex at the foot of it. Like St-Germain-des-Prés, Montparnasse was a quarter associated with writers and artists, who used to hang out at the famous La Coupole restaurant and ballroom (newly renovated), as well as a working-class district. Today it is largely a commercial area with big hotels and office blocks. There are sex shops and clubs in the rue de la Gâité and plenty of cheap restaurants near the Cité University. Near by you will find the entrance to the catacombs on the place Denfert-Rochereau, and the Observatoire. There are many relatively cheap modern hotels in the 15e which tour operators will try to tell you are near the centre. They are not.

THE 13e

No-man's land, the Gare d'Austerlitz, the Chinese quarter (with a market between the avenues de Choisy and d'Ivry) and the Gobelin tapestry factory which you can visit. Much of the area is taken over by tower-block flats where many of the immigrant population live, but there is still some Parisian character around the rue Butte-aux-Cailles with its little bars and bistros. The north of the area is near the 5e.

La Coupole, a brasserie in Montparnasse, has always been popular with Parisian intellectuals, past and present

Museums

For years the ingredients of a trip to Paris were pretty standard: you went to the Louvre, perhaps to the Rodin Museum, to the Notre-Dame Cathedral, up the Eiffel Tower, took a stroll in the Luxembourg gardens and up the Champs-Elysées. If there was time you took a boat ride on the Seine, made a visit to Montmartre, strolled around the Latin Quarter and sat down for a bit to watch the world go by from one of the famous cafés. While you can still do all that, there are some new attractions like the Musée d'Orsay national art gallery and the exciting Cité des Sciences at La Villette, a suburb in the northeast of the capital.

The most popular sights in Paris (in rank order) are: The Pompidou Centre (the Beaubourg), the Eiffel Tower,

The new entrance to the Louvre is through an eye-catching glass pyramid designed by Pei

the Louvre, the Cité des Sciences at La Villette, the Musée d'Orsay, La Géode at La Villette, the Arc de Triomphe and the Musée Picasso.

Most city museums are closed on Monday and free or half-price to all on Sunday. National museums (except the Musée d'Orsay) are shut on Tuesday; under 18s get in free, 18–25-year-olds half-price. For those with only a short time to spend in the city, I have picked out a few of the galleries and museums and divided them into: Essential Viewing and The Rest. Also see The Different Areas (pages 11-20), Landmarks (pages 30-35), Parks, Gardens and Cemeteries (pages 36-41) and Excursions from Paris (pages 41-44).

WHAT TO SEE – MUSEUMS

Essential Viewing

◆◆◆
LOUVRE MUSEUM, *Palais du Louvre, 1er*

Next to the Tuileries Gardens on the Right Bank of the Seine, a former royal palace undergoing massive expansion that will make it the biggest museum in the world by 1992 with even more treasures on display (many of them are at present in the cellars), and escalators to make those mile-long walks down endless corridors less tiring. The glass pyramid, designed by the Chinese-American Pei, at the entrance from Cour Napoléon, is now open, but the excavations will continue for several years. The Ministry of Finance is due to move out to Bercy.

There are seven different museums in the Louvre: Oriental Antiquities, Egyptian Antiquities, Greek and Roman Antiquities, Painting, Sculpture, Furniture and Objets d'art. Top of your list should be Leonardo da Vinci's *Mona Lisa*, the *Winged Victory* and *Venus de Milo*.

There is no possibility of being able to 'do' it all at once, so pick out the works you particularly want to see, and do your best to find them.

Open: 9:00 A.M. to 6:00 P.M. (Monday and Wednesday until 9:45 P.M.) Free on Sundays
Closed: Tuesday
Métro: Palais Royal, Louvre

◆◆◆
MUSÉE D'ORSAY, 7e

1 rue de Bellechasse
Opened at the end of 1986. Impressionist paintings, fine and decorative arts, architecture and photography from 1848 to 1914 (variously moved from the Jeu de Paume, the Palais de Tokyo, and the Louvre) now housed in the spectacularly renovated, airy Gare d'Orsay, the former railway station that served southwest France. A total of 2,300 paintings and 1,500 sculptures. The transformation took ten years.

Go straight to the top, third floor for Impressionist paintings: room upon room of the most famous works of Monet, Renoir, Cézanne, Pissarro, Sisley and Degas. The middle floor exhibits include sculpture by Rodin and Maillol, paintings by Bonnard and Vuillard, works representing Foreign Schools, Symbolism and Naturalism, and Art Nouveau furniture. The ground floor has Decorative Arts 1850–1880 as well as Degas, Manet, Monet and Renoir pre-1870 and a good bookshop in the original buffet. The Café des Hauteurs on the top floor has views through the old station clock over the Seine, and there is an outside terrace to get your breath back. More formal meals are served in the sumptuous first-floor restaurant, with chandeliers, painted ceiling and statues. There are also changing exhibitions, concerts, films and lectures.

Open: 10:00 A.M. to 5.30 P.M. (to 9:15 P.M. Thursday); Sunday 9:00 A.M. to 6:00 P.M.
Closed: Monday
Métro: Solférino, RER ligne C Musée d'Orsay

In the Musée d'Orsay. Van Gogh's jollier pictures appeal to nearly everyone, no matter what their age

◆◆
MUSÉE NATIONAL D'ART MODERNE (National Museum of Modern Art) (better known as the BEAUBOURG or the GEORGES POMPIDOU CENTRE), 4e
Rues Rambuteau, Saint-Martin and Beaubourg
The museum is on the third (1965 to present day) and fourth floor (1905 to 1965) of the Beaubourg centre with changing exhibitions on the 5th floor. A fascinating collection of modern art from Bonnard to Bacon and including works by Rousseau,

Picasso, Matisse, Warhol and Balthus, right up to the present day. There is much going on in the rest of the building (entry is free) which includes a large cinema. There are films on contemporary art, activities for children, an industrial design gallery, a music research unit, and an excellent international arts bookshop.
Open: noon to 10:00 P.M. (weekends 10:00 A.M. to 10:00 P.M.)
Closed: Tuesday
Métro: Rambuteau, Hôtel-de-Ville, RER Châtelet-les-Halles

♦♦♦
MUSÉE PICASSO, *HÔTEL SALÉ*, 3e
5 rue de Thorigny
Until a few years ago the Hôtel Salé, one of the most elegant mansions in the Marais, was in a dilapidated state and occupied by squatters. Today it houses the Picasso Museum and its exterior and splendid interior, including an elegant wrought-iron staircase (one of the finest in Paris), look much as they did in 1656 when Aubert de Fontenay, who made his fortune by levying *la gabelle*, a 'salt' tax (hence the name *salé*), lived there. In between times it was variously a home for rare books at the time of the Revolution, a school, the Venetian Embassy and the official residence of the Archbishop of Paris. As well as many of his lesser-known paintings from his 'blue' period to the 1920s, you can also see Picasso's own collection from his estate including works by Cézanne, Rousseau, Degas and Matisse.
Open: 9:15 A.M. to 5:15 P.M. (Wednesday to 10:00 P.M.)
Closed: Tuesday
Métro: Chemin-Vert, Saint-Paul

LA VILLETTE, 19e
La Villette, in the northeast of Paris just inside the *périphérique* (ring road), is a 136 acre (55 hectare) landscaped park created out of the old abattoirs and surrounded by two canal basins. It stretches from the Porte de la Villette to the Porte de Pantin. It takes about 15 minutes by Métro from central Paris to get there.

The new site includes a variety of venues, the most important of which, if you have children with you, is:

♦♦♦
CITÉ DES SCIENCES ET DE L'INDUSTRIE, 19e
30 avenue Corentin-Cariou
This vast museum encourages children and adults of all ages to learn about Man, Science and Technology through games of discovery. There are several floors, all open-plan with escalators running up to each. It incorporates a Planetarium with an astronomical simulator and a sky of 10,000 stars, an Explora on three levels which focuses on modern day discoveries, and an Inventorium where there are two discovery workshops for different age groups. The only problem is the vast majority of instructions and the commentary at the Planetarium show (extra fee) are in French, although some of the computer games offer an English option and there are headphones to guide you through different areas. On the principle that children never read instructions anyway, however, it should not be beyond most of them to work out how everything works.
In the Inventorium, they can, for example, bicycle alongside their own reflection to show how bones move, work a video telephone with a friend in a nearby booth, or film each other in a TV studio.
The Cité is split into four themes: Earth and the Universe, The Adventure of Life, Matter and Human Labour, Language

and Communication. The surrounding *parc*, which has been ambitiously landscaped, includes a popular dragon slide for younger children.
Open: Tuesday, Thursday and Friday 10:00 A.M. to 6:00 P.M.; Wednesday noon to 9:00 P.M.; Saturday, Sunday and public holidays noon to 8:00 P.M.
Closed: Monday
Métro: see *How to Get There*, below

Also at La Villette:

The Zenith, an enormous, inflatable pop and rock stadium across the canal that seats 6,500. You cannot miss it if you look for a red aeroplane.

The Grande Halle (the old cattle hall) is a huge structure of iron and glass. It has been converted for major concerts and exhibitions.

At the Picasso Museum — housed in a beautiful Marais mansion

La Géode is a huge, mirrored silver globe surrounded by water, behind the Science Museum. Inside there is a 180-degree hemispheric screen for lasers and cinerama-like films. The films are not particularly interesting (in French only) but you feel as if you are part of the setting, as the screen wraps itself around your lateral vision and your ears get used to six-track stereo. Closed Monday.

How to Get There:
Métro: Porte de la Villette. Porte de Pantin Métro is nearer if you are going to Grande Halle only.
By barge: Canauxrama operate cruises along the canal Saint Martin, leaving from the Port de l'Arsenal near the place de la Bastille (*Métro*: Bastille) or from

*La Géode, the revolutionary
hemispheric cinema, at La Villette*

the Bassin de la Villette, quai de
la Loire (*Métro:* Jean-Jaurès).
The journey takes 1½ hours.
Or you can take the Quiztour
barge (April to November) from
central Paris leaving from just
below the Musée d'Orsay from
the quai Anatole France, 7e. You
pass the Louvre and
Notre-Dame *en route*, travel
under the place de la Bastille,
through locks and under swing
bridges to La Villette. The
journey takes three hours and
there is an English commentary.
Information and reservations
Canauxrama, the Bassin de la
Villette, 13 quai de la Loire, 19e.
Tel: 46.07.13.13. Quiztour, 19 rue
d'Athènes, 9e. Tel: 42.40.96.97.

The Rest

◆◆
JEU DE PAUME, 1er
Tuileries Gardens
The Impressionist paintings
have moved to the Musée
d'Orsay and the gallery has
been renovated to house major
exhibitions of 20th-century art.

◆◆
**GRAND PALAIS (NATIONALES
GALERIES), 8e**
*Avenue du Général
Eisenhower,*
Built for the Paris Exhibition in
1900, a huge domed building
with large major exhibitions.
The **Petit Palais** across the
avenue Winston-Churchill has a
permanent collection of
antiques and paintings dating
from antiquity to the beginning

of the 20th century (*Open:* 10.00 A.M. to 5:40 P.M., closed Monday).
Open: 10:00 A.M. to 8:00 P.M. (Wednesday to 10:00 P.M.)
Closed: Tuesday
Metro: Champs-Elysées-Clémenceau

◆
MAISON DE VICTOR HUGO, 4e
6 place des Vosges
Worth a visit if you are at the Picasso Museum. Another insight into a Marais mansion, the house in which Victor Hugo (*Les Misérables*) lived between 1832 and 1848. As well as a writer, he was also a painter and interior decorator and 400 of his paintings as well as replicas of rooms he decorated are on show.
Open: 10:00 A.M. to 5:40 P.M.
Closed: Monday
Métro: Saint-Paul, Bastille, Chemin Vert

◆
MANUFACTURE NATIONALE DES GOBELINS, 13e
42 avenue des Gobelins
Walk south from the Panthéon to the Gobelin factory where you can join a guided tour to see how the famous tapestries are made. Gobelin tapestries are traditionally heavy wall hangings depicting a range of subjects from the seasons to royal lifestyles and residences to designs by great French painters. They are often interwoven with gold, using 17th-century methods.
Open: tours on Tuesday, Wednesday and Thursday afternoons
Closed: rest of the week
Métro: Gobelins

◆◆
MUSÉE D'ART MODERNE DE LA VILLE DE PARIS, 16e
11 avenue du Président-Wilson
Huge building with contemporary works, works of Cubism, the Paris School and Matisse's *Danse* among them. Also Art Deco furniture and changing exhibitions.
Open: 10:00 A.M. to 5:40 P.M. (Wednesday to 8:30 P.M.)
Closed: Monday
Métro: Alma-Marceau, Iéna

The courtyard linking the huge Musée d'Art Moderne and the Palais de Tokyo

◆◆◆
MUSÉE DES ARTS DE LA MODE, 1er
109 rue de Rivoli
Fashion museum in the Pavillon de Marsan in the Palais du Louvre
In the Louvre complex. Four centuries of French fashion on the fifth floor with stunning

displays of fabrics, accessories and costumes, many of them donated by famous names with life-sized mannequins made especially to fit the various outfits. Modern gallery with backlighting, mirrors, porcelain figures and animation to help recreate the times. There is a section of the Orient Express complete with 1920s flappers in sequinned dresses, a theatre of men's fashion and a circus tent with acrobats wearing Schiaparelli boleros. Many temporary exhibitions and a large reference library.
Combine with the **Musée des Arts Decoratifs** (decorative arts and crafts from the Middle Ages until the present day), see below, also part of the Louvre complex.
Open: Wednesday to Saturday 12:30 to 6:00 P.M.; Sunday 11:00 A.M. to 6:00 P.M.
Closed: Monday and Tuesday
Métro: Palais-Royal, Tuileries

◆◆
MUSÉE DES ARTS DÉCORATIFS, 1er
107 rue de Rivoli
On the ground floor. Interior design *à la Français* from the Middle Ages to the present day. Private apartments, tapestries, glass, pottery, paintings and sculpture with a gallery of contemporary design that includes toys and crafts.
Open: Monday to Saturday 12:30 to 6:00 P.M.; Sunday 11:00 A.M. to 6:00 P.M.
Closed: Monday and Tuesday
Métro: Palais-Royal, Tuileries

◆◆
MUSÉE CARNAVALET, 3e
23 rue de Sévigné
History of the city from its origins to the present day. One wing is devoted to the French Revolution.
Open: 10:00 A.M. to 5:40 P.M.
Closed: Monday
Métro: Saint-Paul, Chemin Vert

◆
MUSÉE DE CLUNY, 5e
Hôtel de Cluny
6 place Paul-Painlevé
On the Left Bank, at the crossroads of St-Germain and St-Michel, a group of buildings, including one of three 15th-century houses left in Paris, Roman baths dating from AD 200 and the town residence of the Abbots of Cluny. The museum's galleries contain exhibits from the Middle Ages as well as furniture, sculptures, gold and silver up to the 15th century. It also has several well-known 15th-century tapestries the most perfect example of which is the series of six allegorical hangings known as *The Lady and the Unicorn.*
Open: 9:45 A.M. to 12:30 P.M. and 2:00 P.M. to 5:15 P.M.
Closed: Tuesday
Métro: Odéon, St-Michel

◆
MUSÉE DE L'INSTITUT DU MONDE ARABE, 5e
23 quai Saint-Bernard (entrance in rue des Fossés Saint-Bernard)
On the Left Bank. Worth visiting if you are interested in exhibits of the Arab world and for the architecture. The collection is housed in a modern building opened in 1987 with windows made up of lenses that open and shut with the sun (but do not do anything if it is gray out). Good views from the 9th-floor terrace,

Musée Rodin, where the sculptor lived until he died in 1917, has many of his most famous works in the house and garden

where there is a restaurant.
Open: 1:00 to 8:00 P.M. Free.
Closed: Monday
Métro: Jussieu, Sully-Morland

◆◆
MUSÉE MARMOTTAN
(Académie des Beaux-Arts), 16e
2 rue Louis-Boilly
After the Musée d'Orsay the next best gallery of Impressionist paintings, well worth a visit if you have room for more. A private collection concentrating on Monet, (also Renoir, Gauguin, Manet and Pisarr), alongside

a remarkable collection of Empire-style furniture.
Open: 10:00 A.M. to 5:30 P.M.
Closed: Monday
Métro: La Muette

◆◆
MUSÉE RODIN, 7e
Hôtel Biron, 77 rue de Varenne
Between the Eiffel tower and the Musée d'Orsay, splendid museum in a rococo mansion devoted to Rodin's sculptures including *The Kiss* and *Adam and Eve* with others, including *The Thinker* in the garden.
Open: 10:00 A.M. to 5:15 P.M.
(5:45 P.M. April to September)
Closed: Monday
Métro: Varenne, *RER* Invalides

WHAT TO SEE

◆◆
ORANGERIE DES TUILERIES, 1er

Place de la Concorde
Impressionists up until the 1930s. Famous for the two oval rooms of Monet paintings that include the *Water Lilies.* Also Renoir, Matisse and Picasso.
Open: 9:45 A.M. to 5:15 P.M.
Closed: Tuesday
Métro: Concorde, Tuileries

◆
PALAIS DE TOKYO, 16e

13 avenue du Président-Wilson
The Centre National de la Photographie in the right wing has permanent and temporary photography exhibitions and a Cinémathèque.
Open: 9:45 A.M. to 5:00 P.M.
Closed: Tuesday
Métro: Iéna

The Arc de Triomphe sits squarely at the top of the Champs Elysées, dedicated to the military successes of the armies of Napoleon

Landmarks

Churches and Monuments

◆◆◆
ARC DE TRIOMPHE DE L'ÉTOILE, 8e

Place Charles-de-Gaulle-Étoile
Twelve avenues, including the Champs-Elysées, lead up to this, one of Paris's most familiar monuments, built by Napoleon as a triumphal arch dedicated to the glory of the Imperial army. The names of some 600 generals are inscribed on the walls. The tomb of the unknown soldier reminds the world of the soldiers who died for their country. You can climb to the top for views but they are not as good as those from the Beaubourg or the Eiffel Tower. Cross the road at your peril or view from afar.
Open: October to March 10:00 A.M. to 5:00 P.M., (until 6:00 1 April to 30 September)
Closed: Public holidays
Métro: Charles-de-Gaulle-Étoile

◆◆ CONCIERGERIE, 4e
1 quai de l'Horloge
Ile de la Cité
French history laid bare in a 14th-century Gothic setting. This was where Marie Antoinette awaited her fate (you can see her cell, as well as much evidence of the Revolution, the prisons and the kitchens). Combine with a visit to Notre-Dame, Sainte-Chapelle and the Palais de Justice.
Open: 9:30 A.M. to 6:00 P.M.
Métro: Cité, Châtelet

◆ ÉCOLE MILITAIRE, 7e
Avenue de la Motte-Picquet
A splendid 18th-century building near the Eiffel Tower and les Invalides, the Military Academy, used by the army as an officers' training college. You cannot go in.
Métro: École-Militaire

◆◆◆ EIFFEL TOWER, 7e
Champs de Mars
1,007 feet (307m) high, built as a monument to the Great Exhibition of 1889. It is the queen of Parisian monuments, and to many, the symbol of Paris. You can take an elevator to the viewing platforms (1st, 2nd and 3rd – charge according to level) or climb the 1,710 steps (cheaper) as far as the top from where the views, on a clear day, extend for some 45 miles (72 km). There is an audio-visual of the history of the tower on the first stage, and bars and restaurants including the highly regarded Jules Verne restaurant on the second floor of the south leg, with its own private elevator – one of the very best restaurants in Paris.

Open: 10:00 A.M. to 11:00 P.M. (midnight Friday, Saturday and public holidays, April to early September, and daily in July and August)
Métro: Trocadéro, Bir-Hakeim

◆ LES INVALIDES, (MUSÉE DE L'ARMÉE), 7e
Hôtel National des Invalides
Avenue de Tourville
Built as a home for wounded soldiers by Louis XIV. There are two churches under the famous dome, one contains Napoleon's ashes, the other the tombs of soldiers. There is a collection of weapons in the Army Museum.
Open: 10:00 A.M. to 5:00 P.M. (6:00 in summer)
Métro: Latour-Maubourg, Invalides

◆◆ MADELEINE, 8e
Place de la Madeleine
An unusual looking church dedicated to saint Mary Magdalen, built to look like a Greek temple complete with Corinthian columns. Catholic services are held there.
Métro: Madeleine

◆◆◆ NOTRE-DAME CATHEDRAL, 4e
Ile de la Cité
One of the world's architectural masterpieces, a place of worship since pagan times, completed in the 14th century. An awe-inspiring exterior of Gothic extravagance, with gargoyles, gabled carved doorways and magnificent rose windows. Inside a vast echoing hall, 115 feet (35 m) high, that can hold 9,000 worshippers at any one time. The pillars are

Gothic, the aisles are flanked by chapels and flying buttresses support the roof. If you want to know what is what, tag along behind one of the numerous English-speaking guides or join a tour (10:00 A.M. to 5:00 P.M., 6:00 P.M. April to September).

Notre-Dame Cathedral on the Ile de la Cité, a Gothic masterpiece begun in 1163. There are fine views from the 226ft (69m) tower

You can climb to the top of the towers, stroll in the public garden and visit the museum in the crypt to see the remains of the original cathedral. Outside the west door, on the pavement, *kilomètre zéro* marks the spot from which all distances in France are measured.
Open: 8:00 A.M. to 5:00 P.M. daily
Métro: Cité, *RER* Saint Michel

◆◆
OPÉRA DE PARIS-GARNIER, 9e
8 rue Scribe, Place de l'Opéra
Near the large department stores. Pop in to admire Chagall's wonderful ceiling, the grand staircase and spectacular marble foyer. That is if you do not have tickets for the ballet which is performed here; the opera is now at Opéra-Bastille.
Open: 11:00 A.M. to 5:00 P.M. (depending on rehearsals)
Métro: Opéra

◆
PALAIS DE CHAILLOT, 16e
Place du Trocadéro
Now a theatre (with shows for children), cinema and several galleries and museums including the Musée National des Monuments Français. There are views from the terrace of the gardens, fountains and across towards the Seine and the Eiffel Tower.
Open: (museum) 9:00 A.M. to 6:00 P.M.
Closed: Tuesday
Métro: Trocadéro

◆◆◆
PALAIS DE JUSTICE, 4e
Boulevard du Palais
The Law Courts are on the Île de la Cité, an extravagant series

Sacré Cœur – built by the Catholics of France as a symbol of contrition and hope

of Gothic buildings separated by courtyards and incorporating Sainte-Chapelle. Tours are available. Combine with Notre-Dame Cathedral.
Open: 9:00 A.M. to 5:00 P.M.
Métro: Cité, *RER* Saint Michel

◆
PANTHÉON, 5e
Place du Panthéon
Impressive-looking former church on the highest point on the Left Bank, with a rather disappointing interior housing the 18th- and 19th-century tombs of, among others, Voltaire, Victor Hugo,

Rousseau, Emile Zola and Jean Moulin. You can visit the crypt.
Open: 10:00 A.M. to 12:30 P.M. and 2:00 to 5:30 P.M. (6:00 P.M. in summer)
Métro: Cardinal-Lemoine

◆◆
SACRÉ-COEUR, 18e
35 rue du Chevalier-de-la-Barre
Cupolas topped by an icing sugar dome, famous on Paris's skyline (you can see it from the escalator outside the Georges Pompidou Centre). Built at the end of the 19th century, at the top of Montmartre with views of around 30 miles (48 km) from the dome. The campanile is 262 feet (80 m) high. Catholic visitors from the world over come to

light their candles. Steep climb up or funicular from the Marché Saint-Pierre.
Open: 6:00 A.M. to 11:00 P.M.
Métro: Anvers, Abesses

♦♦♦
SAINTE-CHAPELLE, 1er
Boulevard du Palais
Splendid Gothic architecture with the oldest stained-glass windows in Paris, illustrating the old and new testaments, dating from the 13th century. Combine with Notre-Dame, the Conciergerie and the Palais de Justice.
Open: 9:30 A.M. to 6:15 P.M.
Métro: Cité, *RER* Saint Michel

♦♦
TOUR MONTPARNASSE, 15e
33 avenue du Maine
On the Left Bank. When it was built it was the tallest office building in Europe at 686 feet (209 m) high. Somewhat of an eyesore, it has a restaurant, bar and an observatory on the 56th floor and a further open-air viewing area on the 59th floor with 360-degree views. On a clear day you can see for some 25 miles (40 km). Cheaper than the Eiffel Tower. Free elevator if you go up to the restaurant.
Open: 10:00 A.M. to 10:00 P.M. (11:00 P.M. Friday, Saturday and public holidays, and daily from April to September)
Métro: Montparnasse-Bienvenüe

Squares

♦
PLACE DAUPHINE, 1er
Gravel-filled 17th-century peaceful square with trees, on the Ile de la Cité. You can have tea at Fanny's.
Métro: Cité

♦♦
PLACE DE LA CONCORDE, 8e
The largest and craziest square in Paris with one of Paris's top hotels, the de Crillon, in pride of place. The traffic is frightening. The famous 75ft (23m) high obelisk comes from the Egyptian Temple of Luxor and is covered in hieroglyphics. It is floodlit at night and there are great views up the Champs-Elysées to the Arc de Triomphe. Near the Tuileries Gardens and the Louvre.
Métro: Concorde

♦
PLACE DES VICTOIRES, 2e
Louis XIV architecture and designer boutiques under awnings. No fuss, no frills, just trendy. You may see the designer Kenzo.
Métro: Bourse

♦♦
PLACE DES VOSGES, 4e
In the heart of the restored Marais, the oldest square in Paris and some say the most beautiful, built by Henry IV for festivals and ceremonies and surrounded by elegant mansions or *Hôtels*. Open-air restaurants and antique shops under the arcades. Newly landscaped gardens.
Métro: Chemin Vert

♦♦
PLACE VENDÔME, 1er
Built under Louis XIV, an impressive 17th-century square of great architectural merit with Napoleon on a column overseeing the *haute couture* boutiques and expensive jewellers. In between the Opéra and the Tuileries gardens.
Métro: Tuileries

Parks, Gardens and Cemeteries

Parks and Gardens

◆
BOIS DE BOULOGNE, 16e
On the western edge of Paris running alongside the fashionable 16e. Popular haunt, by night, of prostitutes but safe enough by day. The 2,180 acres (882 hectares) include the famous Longchamp and Auteuil racecourses. There are numerous lakes and ponds for boating, miniature golf and bowling, and bikes for rent. A folk museum, Shakespeare theatre, restaurants, children's playgrounds, outdoor pool and camping possibilities, though heavily booked in summer.
Métro: Porte Dauphine, Porte Maillot, Porte d'Auteuil

◆
BOIS DE VINCENNES, 12e
On the southeast side of Paris in 2,322 acres (940 hectares). Including the Vincennes racecourse, Paris's best zoo, a museum of African and Oceanic art, a château, three boating lakes, restaurants and Punch and Judy show for children. You can also rent bikes.
Métro: St-Mande-Tourelle, Porte-Dorée

◆
JARDIN D'ACCLIMATATION, 16e
On the northern edge of the Bois de Boulogne in 25 acres (10 hectares). *The* park for children, with special attractions during school vacations, on weekends and on Wednesdays during the school year. Range of rides to go on (all priced individually), camel and pony rides, toy trains. Cafés and restaurants.
Métro: Sablons, Porte Maillot

◆◆
JARDIN DES PLANTES, 5e
Botanical garden with more than 10,000 classified plants, maze and small zoo in 70 acres (28 hectares). Also winter garden with rare flora from the Alps, the Pyrénées and the North Pole. There are several natural history museums, including Musée National de l'Histoire Naturelle (57 rue Cuvier), with fossils, minerals, anatomy and paleontology, plus changing art exhibitions.
Open: 10:00 A.M. to 5:00 P.M.
Closed: Tuesdays. Entrance fee.
Métro: Gare d'Austerlitz, Jussieu

◆
JARDIN DES SERRES D'AUTEUIL, 16e
Rare arboretum. Ninety-four hothouses with rare tropical plants, 140 varieties of camellia, orchids, palmarium.
Open: 10:00 A.M. to 5:00 P.M. (6:00 P.M. March to September)
Métro: Porte d'Auteuil

◆◆◆
JARDIN DU LUXEMBOURG, 6e
Choose this or the Tuileries for your Sunday afternoon stroll. Sixty-two acres (26 hectares) against a backdrop of the Palais du Luxembourg built for Marie de'Medici, Henry IV's widow, to remind her of the Palazzo Pitti and Boboli Gardens in Florence. Watch little Parisians sail their boats on the pond, old men play *boules* and linked-armed lovers stroll the tree-lined avenues. Keep off the grass.
RER: Luxembourg

Parc de Bagatelle, known for its roses, irises and water lilies

♦♦♦
JARDIN DES TUILERIES, 1er

Opposite the place de la Concorde. Sixty acres (24 hectares) designed by Le Nôtre stretching from the place de la Concorde to the place du Carrousel, including a splendid Orangerie which houses temporary exhibitions and the Jeu de Paume museum, now renovated to house major temporary exhibitions of 20th-century art. A mini Arc de Triomphe built in 1805 commemorates Napoleon's victories, smaller than the real one which you can see by taking the path through the centre of the gardens.
Métro: Tuileries, Concorde

♦♦
JARDIN MUSÉE RODIN, 7e
77 rue Varenne
Well worth a visit for its 2,000 rose bushes and copies of world-famous sculptures by Rodin, as well as the house.
Open: Wednesday to Sunday 10:00 A.M. to 5:15 P.M. (5:45 P.M. April to September)
Closed: Monday and Tuesday
Métro: Varenne, *RER* Invalides

♦
PARC DE BAGATELLE, 16e
Sixty acres (24 hectares) of the Bois de Boulogne with rose gardens (international exhibition 1 to 30 June), tulip exhibitions (mid-March to mid-April), hundreds of water lilies, a pond and a restaurant.
Open: 9:00 A.M. to 6:00 P.M.
Métro: Pont de Neuilly

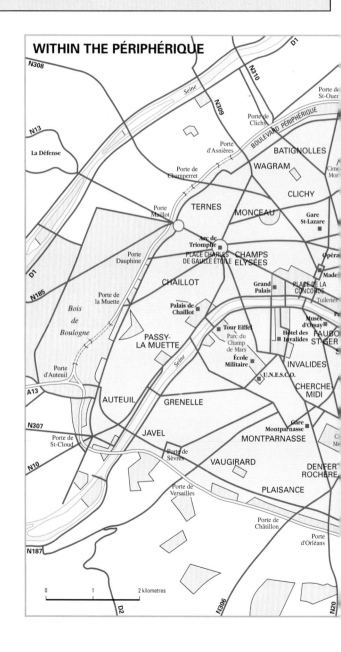

WITHIN THE PÉRIPHÉRIQUE

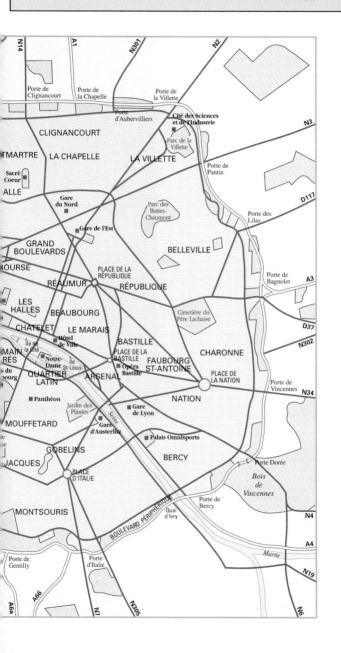

◆
PARC DES BUTTES-CHAUMONT, 19e

In the north of Paris, 67 acres (27 hectares) including a lake and waterfall, children's playground, two restaurants and a café. There are splendid views from the little temple in the lake across to Sacré-Cœur in Montmartre.
Métro: Buttes-Chaumont, Botzaris

◆
PARC MONCEAU, 17e

Boulevard de Courcelles
Twenty three acres (9 hectares) of 18th-century gardens with pagodas. Pleasantly wooded nanny territory with children's playground and sandpit. Also roller-skating rink.
Métro: Monceau

Cemeteries

You may wonder why on earth you would want to include a visit to a cemetery on your Paris itinerary but the graves and tombstones of artists, writers and celebrities, and not just French ones, are fascinating, the sculptures on the tombs are works of art, and the grounds themselves are a peaceful retreat from the bustle of city life.

◆
THE MONTMARTRE CEMETERY, 18e

20 avenue Rachel
The last resting place of Dumas, the composers Offenbach and Berlioz, Emile Zola (though his remains are in the Panthéon) and Degas. You can wander through part of it if you are walking up to Sacré-Cœur.
Métro: Blanche

◆
THE MONTPARNASSE CEMETERY, 14e

3 boulevard Edgar Quinet
Laid out in 1824. Tombs of Sartre, Baudelaire, and Guy de Maupassant.
Métro: Edgar Quinet

◆◆
PÈRE LACHAISE CEMETERY, 20e

Boulevard de Ménilmontant
Père Lachaise is Paris's largest cemetery with some stunning sculptures and beautiful tombs packed fairly closely together in

Parc Monceau was designed to look like a late 18th-century English and German garden

tree-lined avenues, including a moving Monument for the Dead, built in 1900. Among the cast list of celebrities buried there are: Molière, Balzac, Bellini, Chopin, Bizet, Oscar Wilde, Proust, the actress Sarah Bernhardt, Edith Piaf and singer Jim Morrison of The Doors. You should ask the custodian for a plan of the grounds to help identify the tombs.
Métro: Père Lachaise

Excursions from Paris

There are many worthwhile places to visit within a few hours' travelling time from Paris. Most can be reached by public transportation. You can also join bus tours, with a guide, if you do not mind having to keep up with the pace or paying a great deal more than the cost of getting there independently. Some of the tours cover more than one place in an afternoon.
The main places to visit are:

◆◆
CHARTRES
Wonderful cathedral city, with the huge Gothic 13th-century Cathedral of Notre-Dame itself (the nave is the widest in France and the crypt the largest) the main reason for a visit. Eighty-eight miles (142 km) from Paris. Five-and-a-half-hour bus tours include a guided tour of the Cathedral. Or train from Gare de Montparnasse (every 60 mins).

◆◆
FONTAINEBLEAU
Renaissance palace in the middle of a forest with French and Italian interior: Gobelins tapestries, frescoes, and paintings. You can visit the apartments where Louis XIII was born and the *petits appartements* of Napoleon and Josephine. In Josephine's bedroom there are silk wall hangings and matching chairs and curtains that took a workshop in Lyon 20 years to reproduce. The recently opened **Musée Napoléon** in the Louis XV wing of the building has a collection

donated to the State by the Royal Family with paintings, china and furniture.
Reached by train from Gare de Lyon (50 mins).
Open: 9:30 A.M. to 12:30 P.M. and 2:00 to 5:00 P.M.
Closed: Tuesday
See also pages 48-51 for the Forest of Fontainebleau.

The Renaissance château of Fontainebleau, with its splendid English garden and parterre

◆◆
GIVERNY
Small village in southeast Normandy, Claude Monet's home. You can see the landscape that inspired one of France's greatest Impressionist painters, his home, studio and gardens, with the magnificent lily pond and famous Japanese bridge. Five-hour bus tours

available. Or train from St-Lazare to Vernon (50 mins) and then bus to Giverny.
Open: April to October. Gardens 10:00 A.M. to 6:00 P.M., house from 10:00 A.M. to noon and 2:00 to 6:00 P.M.
Closed: Monday

◆◆
MALMAISON
Napoleon's château bought for Josephine. Tours, in French only, take about an hour and a quarter. Tiny compared to Versailles or Fontainebleau (see those first). The Museum contains the Bonapartes' possessions as well

as items from the Tuileries, St-Cloud and Fontainebleau. Josephine's apartments include her jewellery and perfumes and bills for her dresses. After her death it was discovered that she owed three million francs. Lovely gardens and a park to walk around. Five and a half miles (9 km) from Porte Maillot. Three and a half-hour bus tours available. Or the RER from Charles-de-Gaulle-Étoile to La Défense (5 mins), the 158A bus (25 mins), then walk (10 mins). *Open:* 10:00 A.M. to 1:00 P.M. and 1:30 to 5:50 P.M. Free on Wednesday
Closed: Tuesday

◆◆
SAINT-CLOUD

Park in a residential suburb on the south bank of the Seine, designed by Le Nôtre as part of a royal residence. Near the Pasteur Institute. Good views of Paris from the Rond Point de la Balustrade, fountains, terraces and Trocadéro garden and **Musée Historique** (Wednesday, Saturday and Sunday 2:00 to 6:00 P.M.; 5:00 P.M. in winter). Two miles (3 km) from Porte de St-Cloud, west of Paris. *Métro:* Boulogne-Porte de St-Cloud (last stop, line 10)

◆◆
SAINT-DENIS

Visited mainly for its 12th-century Gothic Cathedral (the model for Chartres), burial place of many kings and queens of France, as well as Saint Denis, a third-century evangelist who kept on walking after he had been decapitated in Montmartre. You can see archaeological exhibits and medieval ceramics in the **Musée d'Art et d'Histoire**, rue Gabriel-Peri (open 10:00 A.M. to 5:30 P.M., Sunday 2:00 P.M. to 6:00 P.M.; closed Tuesday). Six miles (9 km) from Porte de la Chapelle on the motorway. Or métro to Saint-Denis-Basilique (line 13 from St-Lazare).

◆◆
SAINT-GERMAIN-EN-LAYE

If you have time to spare, worth visiting for the Renaissance château which houses the **Musée Antiquités Nationales**. The attractive grounds have a Grande Terrasse designed by Le Nôtre. Nearby woods for picnicing. Priory to visit. Nine miles (14 km) from Porte Maillot. Train to Saint-Germain-en-Laye. *Museum open:* 9:45 A.M. to noon and 1:30 to 5:15 P.M.
Closed: Tuesdays

◆◆
SÈVRES

For lovers of pottery and ceramics. The famous multi-coloured **Musée National de la Céramique** which contains samples as well as porcelain from around the world. Two miles (3 km) from Porte de St-Cloud.
Métro: Pont-de-Sèvres
Open: 10:00 A.M. to noon and 1:30 to 5:15 P.M.
Closed: Tuesday

◆◆
LES TRIANONS

See Versailles below.

◆◆◆
VERSAILLES

If you have to choose one place to visit outside Paris, make it this one. Allow plenty of time. Unfortunately it is always crowded, especially on Sundays

Versailles, home of 17th and 18th-century French kings, and model for other Royal residences

when the entrance fee is reduced. The Michelin Green guide devotes 13 pages to Louis XIII's sumptuous château, made even grander by Louis XIV (to house 3,000 courtiers) with the help of Le Brun, Le Vau and Le Nôtre who landscaped the gardens. Most people do not have time to see everything. There are guided tours available. Priorities should be: the 246ft (75m) long Hall of Mirrors, the most famous room in the palace, although the glass is not original; the State Apartments; the white and gold Chapel (all of which you can see without a guide) and the gardens (which are free). If you visit on a summer Sunday the fountains may be on (check with the Tourist Office for specific dates and times) otherwise the statues look a bit sad. You can stroll along the formal terraces and parterres, see the Orangery and numerous statues, and find relative peace as you wander further away from the Palace. There are always renovations going on at Versailles (which might close one or more galleries). The renovated apartments of the Dauphin and Dauphiness and of Louis XV's daughters are now open.

◆◆
LES TRIANONS are lesser palaces. The **Grand Trianon** is lavish with a pink marbled façade, the **Petit Trianon** less so. You get there by walking from the Neptune Gate along the avenue de Trianon.

Versailles is 8 miles (13 km) from Porte d'Auteuil. Three-and-a-half hour, and longer, escorted bus tours are available. Train from Les Invalides to Versailles Rive Gauche (takes half an hour). *Open:* 9:45 A.M. to 5:00 P.M. *Closed:* Monday Reduced prices on Sundays but hardly worth it as you may have to wait in line.

Wildlife and Countryside in and around Paris
by Paul Sterry

France's capital city lies on a low-lying basin known as the Ile de France which is dominated by the meandering Seine. In the hills surrounding the basin, the French aristocracy built splendid châteaux surrounded by parks and formal gardens. At the time they were built, each was sited in its own tract of woodland, maintained for private hunting.

Despite recent urban sprawl, most of the château woodlands have remained more or less intact to this day. Were it not for the private and in some cases formerly royal status of the forests, the Paris basin would undoubtedly have lost much more of its woodland to development than it has.

Not surprisingly, most of the wildlife interest of the Ile de France is also associated with woodland, which would after all have been the dominant vegetation before man's influence was fully felt. Woods as close as 12 miles (20 km) to Paris have plenty to offer, but to see lowland forest at its best you must travel south to Fontainebleau (see pages 41, 48-49). This forest is not only good by the standards of the Paris basin but is also one of the finest in the whole of France.

Parks and Formal Gardens
In terms of wildlife interest, the centre of Paris is much like any other European city. The inevitable pigeons and house sparrows congregate wherever there is a meal to be

had and, in the winter, starlings roost on some of the city's buildings.

Within the city itself, the Bois de Boulogne is, in spring and summer, a leafy park modelled on London's Hyde Park. Although scenically attractive, there is little natural vegetation within its boundaries because it was replanted with acacias and sycamores after Napoleon's troops wrecked the native oak woodland in 1815. You should also be warned that it has a reputation for being unsafe after dark so enjoy it during the daylight hours.

Almost all the châteaux surrounding Paris have formal gardens, many of which are open to the public and some, such as Ermenonville, have English-style parkland as well. The most famous of all Paris's formal gardens are those surrounding the Palais de Versailles, 15 miles (25 km) south of Paris on the A13. However, the gardens at Chantilly, famous for its pastries and lace, although on a more modest scale are equally attractive.

The Bois de Boulogne lies on the western edge of Paris, alongside the Périphérique. Tracks, paths, woodland and lakes provide wildlife and scenic interest and, within its boundaries, the Parc de Bagatelle is renowned for its rose gardens and floral displays. The 2,322 acre Bois de Vincennes, to the southeast of Paris, harbours the zoo, the Vincennes racecourse and formal gardens. Woodland and parkland birds can be found here, especially in spring and summer.

PEACE AND QUIET

Checklist of common birds in parks and gardens:

mallard *R*
black-headed gull *R*
woodpigeon *R*
swallow *S*
white wagtail *R*
dunnock *R*
robin *R*
blackbird *R*
song thrush *R*
blue tit *R*
great tit *R*
chaffinch *R*
house sparrow *R*

R year-round resident
S summer visitor

Rivers and Lakes

Most of the rivers, lakes and ponds in and around the centre of Paris are either man-made or have been changed significantly from their natural state. Lakes like the one in the Bois de Boulogne are too ornamental and disturbed to hold anything more than wild ducks and geese, swans and black-headed gulls.

In the forests and farmland surrounding the city, however, there are plenty of natural and semi-natural water bodies, supporting water-loving plants and animals, each acting like a magnet to the wildlife of the surrounding land. The Forest of Chantilly contains natural lakes known as les Etangs de Comelle, and there are numerous woodland pools and lakes in the Forests of Ermenonville and Rambouillet. The richest and most extensive areas of wetland are found within the Forest of Fontainebleau.

The Kingfisher

Kingfishers are without doubt the most colourful bird that visitors are likely to see around Paris: the plumage comprises a mixture of orange-red and several shades of blue. They are invariably found near water and often perch on overhanging branches.

Kingfishers are master fishermen, diving into the water to catch small fish. These are dispatched by a swift blow against the perch and either swallowed whole or fed to their young during the breeding season.

Kingfishers nest in burrows excavated into banks. At the end of the breeding season, the burrow is a smelly mess of droppings and fish bones.

Lake in the Bois de Boulogne

Checklist of wildlife thay may be seen around freshwater:

kingfisher   R
grey heron   R
sand martin   S
swallow   S
pochard   W
tufted duck   W
moorhen   R
coot   R
black tern   S
reed warbler   S
dragonflies   S
mayflies   S
yellow iris   S
water lily   S

R   year round resident
S   present in summer only
W   most frequently seen in
      winter

Château Forests

The châteaux, which ring the outskirts of Paris at a discreet distance, were once the homes of the French nobility. They catered to their every need and so, in addition to the grand houses and formal gardens, most of them had private forests devoted to the nobility's main outdoor pursuit — hunting. Nowadays, many of these woodlands are open to the public, or at least can be viewed when visiting the château. Despite their proximity to Paris, they hold a wide variety of interesting wildlife. The Forest of Marly, on either side of the A13 autoroute to Normandy, has glades through oak, beech and sweet chestnut woodland, and roe deer are sometimes seen on the forest rides. There are also pleasant woodland walks through the Forest of St-Germain, 15 miles (25 km) northwest of Paris on the N13. Situated near St-Germain-en-laye, the birthplace of Debussy, the elevation of the forest affords excellent views of the meandering Seine.

Red squirrels can be seen throughout France. Although pinewoods are the preferred habitat of these agile climbers, the less disturbed beechwoods of the Paris basin harbour these charming animals.

Although not as rich as the Forest of Fontainebleau (see pages 48-49, 50-51), the woods around Versailles, Chantilly and Rambouillet still hold some of the region's special birds, notably middle-spotted woodpecker and short-toed

PEACE AND QUIET

treecreeper. Versailles lies 15 miles (25km) south of Paris on the A13, Rambouillet is southwest of Paris on the D906 and Chantilly is north of Paris on the N16.

Insect life is most abundant in the summer. The air is sometimes filled with the audible buzzing of flies and bees and several species of bush-cricket chirp from the foliage along tracks and paths. Woodland rides are also the haunt of butterflies as they seek out flowers or shafts of sunlight. Speckled woods occur from May to September and are true sun-worshippers, spending hours on end basking in the heat. They are extremely territorial insects and will vigorously fight off intruders of the same species. Speckled woods are grey-brown in colour

In spring, beechwoods around Paris are full of bird song

with paler speckled markings on both the upper and lower wings. Their caterpillars feed on various grasses.

Fontainebleau

Of all the woodlands of the Paris basin, Fontainebleau is by far the most outstanding. With over 1,200 species of flowering plant recorded within its boundaries, 20 of which are orchids, it is one of the finest lowland forests in the whole of France. Fontainebleau has the advantage over many woodlands in other parts of France of having open public access. Although driving is restricted to the lanes and roads, you can walk anywhere along the leafy tracks and paths, some of which are signposted routes, and discover secret glades and clearings. It is also easily reached from Paris, being less than 44 miles (70 km) to the south along the N7 and with frequent train services from the centre. The charming village of Barbizon is perhaps one of the most attractive starting points from which to explore the area. Although most parts of the 61,750 acre (25,000 hectare) Forest of Fontainebleau are rewarding, and marked trails and paths abound, the Gorges de Franchard is an outstanding area. The French Ordnance Survey produce a map to the *Forêt de Fontainebleau*, (number 401). The scale of 1:25,000 should enable you to find your bearings and not get lost.

The secret of Fontainebleau's richness lies in its variety of habitats, this in turn a result of

The crested tit is a year-round woodland resident

the different types of soil and bedrock found in the region. Extensive beech woods favour the lime-rich areas while oak and birch are dominant on acid soils. Patches of heathland can be found on dry sandy soils, and in wetter areas the heath merges into bog. Where the soil is less acid, fenland and marshland vegetation predominate. To complete the variety, there are dramatic outcrops and gorges of both sandstone and limestone, some large enough to provide weekend practice sites for climbing enthusiasts. Fontainebleau is big enough and varied enough to have wild boar roaming its more secluded areas. You would be lucky to see *them*, but the deer which are also here should be easier to spot! As might be expected in such an exciting area, the birdlife is very rich, a roll-call of species that would do credit to northern and eastern Europe.

Woodland Birds

The further away from Paris you travel, the richer the woodland birdlife becomes and particularly in the forests around Fontainebleau.

In the spring, undisturbed patches of woodland come alive with birdsong. Nightingales and blackcaps are common in suitable habitat and compete with a variety of other warblers. The beautiful descending trill of the willow warbler is heard from open patches of birch and willow whilst wood warblers frequent stands of ancient beech. The song of the latter is a distinctive trill which speeds up as it goes along, and has been likened to a small coin spinning on a metal plate!

If you are very fortunate, you may hear France's most colourful woodland bird, the golden oriole, colourful both in terms of song and appearance.

PEACE AND QUIET

The song consists of a series of loud flute-like whistles, reminiscent of something from a tropical forest. Although the bird itself is bright yellow, it remains hidden in the tree canopy and is seldom seen.

Fontainebleau's Woodpeckers

The Forest of Fontainebleau is one of the few places in Europe where you stand a reasonable chance of seeing six species of woodpecker in a single visit. Its fame has spread far and wide and birdwatchers are known to make the pilgrimage to Fontainebleau specifically to search for woodpeckers.

The best time of year to search for woodpeckers is in late winter, before there are any leaves on the trees to obscure your view, and when the birds begin calling at the start of the breeding season. Since they all have distinctive, and often loud, calls and 'drum' with their beaks on tree trunks, they are easily located by tracking the source of the sound.

Three of the woodpecker species have black, white and red plumages in varying amounts. The sparrow-sized lesser-spotted woodpecker has neat black and white barring on its back, distinct from the two larger species which have a conspicuous white patch on each wing. To separate these two you must look carefully at their heads. Middle-spotted woodpeckers always have a bright red cap and white cheeks whilst adult great-spotteds always have a black cap and a black cheek stripe.

Violets in early spring

The green woodpecker will already be familiar to many visitors with its green plumage, yellow rump and loud yelping call, known as 'yaffling'. However, in Fontainebleau you should look at each one you see carefully because its close relative, the grey-headed woodpecker, also occurs in the more open parts of the woodland. As its name implies, it has a grey head and lacks the extensive red crown of the green woodpecker.

The real prize of the Forest of Fontainebleau is the black

woodpecker. This is Europe's largest woodpecker, the size of a crow, with jet-black plumage. Although occasionally located by sight alone, the best way to find one is to listen for its far-carrying flutey call, quite unlike any other woodpecker, or its extremely loud drumming.

Woodland Flowers
Springtime in Paris itself is legendary, but it is also, of course, a delightful time to visit the Paris woodlands. Before the leaves are fully formed on the trees, dappled light filters through the canopy to the woodland floor. The spring is the best growing period for most woodland flowers because there is still plenty of light before the canopy shades it out. Many wither and die back by the time summer comes. Wood sorrel, with its delicate white flowers and shamrock leaves, often forms carpets on the woodland floor, with patches of common dog violets adding a splash of mauve and the flowers of wood anemones nodding in the slightest woodland breeze. Large patches of anemones with their large, dissected leaves and striking flowers can give the impression of a well-cared-for garden border

PEACE AND QUIET

plant rather than a wild flower. In more open areas, particularly in clearings and along tracks, you may come across the showy spikes of early purple orchids with glossy, spotted leaves. This is generally the first orchid to appear in the woods around Paris, and is often in flower in the first week of May. It is followed by many other species later in the year and, in the Forest of Fontainebleau in particular, up to 20 species occur.

In the deep shade of beech woods look for the bird's nest orchid, one of the less showy species found in the region, but nevertheless one with a fascinating way of life. This curious straw-coloured plant, which grows up to 1 foot (30 cm) tall, has no leaves and is almost entirely lacking in chlorophyll, the pigment which gives plants their green colour.

Highlights of the woodland year:

Spring
Migrant warblers arrive.
Woodland bird singing to advertise breeding territory.
Nightingales singing at dusk.
Woodpeckers excavating nests.
Spring flowers carpet the woodland floor.
A succession of wild orchids.
Colourful new growth of leaves.

Summer
Family parties of birds moving noisily through the trees.
Sparrowhawks circling over the woodland canopy.
Butterflies such as speckled wood, purple hairstreak and white admiral appear.
Insects such as beetles and flies in abundance.
Squirrels with young.

Autumn
The leaves begin to change colour – shades of yellow and brown predominate.
Berries, fruits and nuts are produced in abundance.
Squirrels and jays gathering acorns on the woodland floor.
Colourful fungi appear.
Deer rutting at the start of the mating season.

Winter
Woodland birds such as chaffinches form flocks.
Fieldfares, redwings and bramblings arrive as winter visitors to the woodlands.
Winter fungi appear.
Lichens, mosses and ferns seen well with no leaves on the trees.
Small mammals forage on the ground.

Woodland Mammals

The forests surrounding the Paris basin were once the hunting preserves of the French nobility. The original quarry animals still survive and the deer, for example, are still occasionally hunted.

Deer occur in woods as close to Paris as Versailles, but the best place to see them is in the Forest of Fontainebleau, further south. Red deer are the largest species found in this part of France, the stags with their branched, spiky antlers. Listen for the loud, cough-like bark with which they signal danger to others.

The smaller fallow deer has beautiful, dappled fur in the summer and the males have broad, flattened antlers. Both fallow and red deer are herd animals and have a distinct rutting season in the autumn.

A magnificent red deer stag

Dominant stags defend a harem of females from intruding males and their loud bellowing calls carry a long way on a misty October morning. Both fallow and red deer produce their young in the late spring. The dappled fawns and calves, as they are respectively known, are well camouflaged against the woodland floor. If you come across one please do not touch it because your scent may cause its mother to desert it when she returns.

The smallest deer found in the woods around Paris is the tiny roe deer. Their rutting season is in July and August when their coats are a warm red colour. You might hear their piping and barking calls while on an early morning walk through the woods. By December, when they shed their antlers, their coat has become grey-brown. This blends in with the surrounding vegetation extremely well, but when they run they have a conspicuous white patch around the tail. One of the noisiest of the woodland's inhabitants is the wild boar which forages loudly in the woodland floor and frequently snorts. For all its apparent brashness, it can be difficult to see, crashing off through the undergrowth at the first sign of danger.

Harvest from the Fields and Forests

The French have a passion for fungi. Mushrooms and toadstools of all sorts feature heavily in French cuisine and there are whole markets

PEACE AND QUIET

devoted to them with a vast range of species offered for sale.

Of course, if you want the freshest fungi of all, you have to go and pick them yourself and autumn fungus forays are a popular Parisian pursuit in the woods and fields surrounding the capital. However, identifying some of the choicest species takes considerable skill so for the casual observer perhaps the best advice is to look and admire but do not touch.

Fields and grassland are the traditional site for the field mushroom, the wild ancestor of the most familiar of all edible fungi. However, stately parasol mushrooms, which sometimes grow in large groups, are equally prized. But in terms of weight and size there is nothing to beat the giant puffball which can grow to a size of 2 feet (60 cm) in diameter. This species is particularly delicious coated in egg and breadcrumbs and deep-fried.

With all fungi it is essential to pick them when they are just at their best. This is certainly the case with the giant puffball. A day or two too late and all you are left with is a giant bag of spores!

Woodlands offer a greater variety of mushrooms and toadstools than fields. The 'cep' or penny bun, which has pores instead of gills under its cap, is one of the most popular species in French kitchens and is commonly found under birch trees.

Fungi come in all shapes and sizes, not just the conventional 'mushroom' shape. Two of the tastiest are funnel-shaped with gills on the outside. At first glance the horn of plenty is rather dark and unappealing and is certainly difficult to spot amongst the dead leaves on the woodland floor. Since it dries well, it is often kept to flavour stews and soups. The chanterelle, on the other hand, looks as good as it tastes, being an attractive orange colour with a sharp smell of apricots.

Do not expect to find the most famous and most expensive of France's fungi, the truffle, quite so easily. They lie buried deep beneath the soil and require the nose of a trained dog to locate them.

Sites of Peace and Quiet:
Forêt de Fontainebleau – extensive woodland with a wealth of birds and flowers. Something of interest throughout the year.
Bois de Boulogne – woodland birds and rose gardens of the Parc de Bagatelle.
Bois de Vincennes – parkland birds and pleasant strolls.
Forêt de Chantilly – mixed woodland, good for walks.
Forêt de Rambouillet – mixed woodland, good for walks.
Forêt de Marly – mixed woodland.
Forêt de Versailles – especially good for birds. Something of interest throughout the year.
Jardin des Plantes – botanical garden, best in spring and summer.
Jardin de Luxembourg – parkland.
Jardin de Tuileries – parkland.

SHOPPING

Parisian women of all ages stand out a mile whether dressed in exclusive *haute couture* or the stylish garb of a student. Their elegant, chic appearance makes most visitors feel their own wardrobe could do with a revamp, so shopping for clothes, or at least accessories, takes on a pressing importance.

Paris shop windows are exhibition pieces in themselves. It is almost impossible to walk past the tempting window displays of the *confisseries, pâtisseries* and *charcuteries* as well as the shops selling perfumes and lingerie. While shopping in Paris *can* cost the earth, if you know where to go it need not be at all expensive. Some salons and boutiques shut on Mondays, although the main department stores are open.

The old Les Halles market is now a modern underground shopping centre called the Forum

The Main Areas

Although Paris is not very large, you might like to concentrate your shopping, particularly if you are short of time, on one area.

If you want to buy clothes, the most exclusive fashion houses are in the 8e on the Right Bank *(Rive Droit)*. There are, of course, more reasonably priced designer boutiques all over Paris, with a concentration on the Left Bank in and around St-Germain-des-Prés. If you do not mind shopping underground, there are numerous boutiques in the Forum des Halles near the Beaubourg. All the main designers are also represented in Galeries Lafayette.

SHOPPING

Antiques

The equivalent of Sotheby's is the New Drouot at 9 rue Drouot, 9e (11:00 A.M. to 6:00 P.M., closed Sundays). There are three floors with several salesrooms. Anyone can have a look.

It is also well worth browsing in the beautiful arcaded Le Louvre des Antiquaires (2 place du Palais Royal, 1er) opposite the Louvre, where 250 dealers offer a range of quality antiques from French furniture to jewellery. Open daily from 11:00 A.M. to 7:00 P.M. (closed Monday all year and Sundays in summer from mid-July to mid-September). Otherwise there are antique shops on the Right Bank; on the Ile St Louis; in the nearby Marais; on the Ile de la Cité and in the rue du Faubourg-Saint-Honoré in the 8e. And on the Left Bank, in the rue du Bac 7e, the rue Jacob 6e, and around the rue de l'Université 7e.

You can buy old prints and postcards from the booksellers on the *quais* along the banks of the Seine.

Department Stores

Most of the department stores are on the Right Bank near the Opéra and the Hôtel de Ville. Au Bon Marché is on the Left. Many of the stores are spread over several buildings.

Galeries Lafayette, 40 boulevard Haussmann, 9e, is possibly the most up-market and sophisticated (there is also a branch in the Montparnasse Shopping Centre). Both branches have an excellent range of top designer clothes for men, women and children as well as their own labels, good ideas for gifts, jewellery and kitchen gadgets. There are good views of Paris from the top-floor roof terrace.

Printemps, at 64 boulevard Haussmann 9e, claims to be the most Parisian — it is over 100 years old. The perfume hall is vast, and the store devotes a large amount of space to design and home furnishings. It too has excellent views from the roof terrace (with a multi-nationality self-service restaurant under the stained-glass dome) on the top floor. There are other branches. Two of the oldest department stores are **Au Bon Marché** in the rue du Bac/rue de Sèvres, 7e on the Left Bank (worth visiting for its selection of perfumes, linens and sensible household

Galeries Lafayette is one of several department stores on the Right Bank

equipment) and **La Samaritaine** on the rue de Rivoli and rue de la Monnaie in the 1er, a vast store that claims to sell virtually everything from maids' uniforms to pets. Their roof terrace bar on the 10th floor of Magasin 2 is open from April to September.

The **Bazar de L'Hôtel de Ville** further down the rue de Rivoli, 4e is also huge and not terribly interesting for visitors as its main claim to fame is Do-It-Yourself, though they do stay open until 10:00 P.M. on Wednesdays if you fancy some late night shopping.

Aux Trois Quartiers, in the boulevard de la Madeleine, 1er is a less exciting alternative. Many department stores also have a food section.

Prisunic (52 avenue des Champs-Elysées, 8e and branches) or the first floor of

Monoprix next to Printemps in boulevard Haussmann are both good for take-home shopping: wine, French mustard, cheese, coffee, chocolate, perhaps a garlic press. Monoprix and **Prisunic** are also the cheapest places to buy things for children, household items, underwear, accessories and costume jewellery.

Tax: If you spend over a certain amount, you can get a tax refund of 13 or 18 per cent which is forwarded to your home address if you keep all the relevant receipts (see Tax under Directory page 118) and get the forms stamped at Customs.

Opening hours: Department stores open from 9:30 A.M. until 6:30 P.M. and Wednesday is late night shopping (until 8:00 or 10:00 P.M.). If you get stuck there are information desks in most of them and generally more helpful assistants than in some of the smaller boutiques.

Fashion

Haute couture and famous designer labels (Chanel, Cardin, Balmain, Dior and the like) can be found in the 8e and the 1er *arrondissements,* particularly along the avenue Montaigne and the lower end of the rue du Faubourg-St-Honoré near the Elysée Palace. The avenue Victor Hugo and the avenue Marceau in the 16e also have exclusive salons. While prices for complete outfits can be astronomical, you can pick up reasonably priced accessories. For *prêt à porter* (off-the-rack-items) the Left Bank is full of fashion boutiques. Most

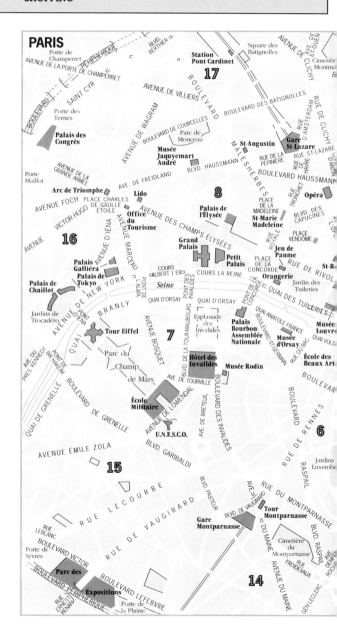

PARIS

Porte de
Champerret
AVENUE DE LA PORTE DE CHAMPERRET
BLVD. BERTHIER
Square des
Batignolles
AVENUE DE CLICHY
AVE. DE ST-OUEN
Cimetièr
Montma

**Station
Pont Cardinet**

17

SAINT CYR
Porte des
Ternes
BOULEVARD
AVENUE DE VILLIERS
BOULEVARD
BOULEVARD DES BATIGNOLLES
RUE D'AMSTERDAM
RUE DE CLICHY

**Palais des
Congrès**

Porte
Maillot
AVENUE DE LA
GRANDE ARMÉE
AVENUE DE WAGRAM
BOULEVARD DE COURCELLES
Parc de
Monceau
**Musée
Jaquemart
André**
St-Augustin
RUE DE LA
PEPINIERE
RUE ST-LAZARE
RUE DE LA HAVRE
**Gare
St-Lazare**

BLVD. HAUSSMANN
BOULEVARD HAUSSMANN
RUE TRONCHET
RUE TRONCHET

Arc de Triomphe
AVE. DE FREIDLAND
MALESHERBES
PLACE
DE LA
MADELEINE
Opéra

AVENUE FOCH
PLACE CHARLES
DE GAULLE
ÉTOILE
Lido
AVENUE DES CHAMPS ÉLYSÉES
**Palais de
l'Elysée**
**St-Marie
Madeleine**
BLVD. DES
CAPUCINES

VICTOR HUGO
**Office
du
Tourisme**
RUE ROYALE
PLACE
VENDÔME

AVENUE
AVENUE D'IÉNA
AVENUE MARCEAU
**Grand
Palais**
**Jeu de
Paume**
St-R

16
COURS
ALBERT 1 ER
**Petit
Palais**
PLACE
DE LA
CONCORDE
RUE DE RIVOL

**Palais
Galliéra**
**Palais de
Tokyo**
Seine
COURS LA REINE
Orangerie
Jardin des
Tuileries
QUAI DES TUILERIES

**Palais de
Chaillot**
PONT DE
L'ALMA
QUAI D'ORSAY
QUAI D'ORSAY
QUAI ANATOLE FRANCE
**Musée
Louvre**
QUAI VOLTA

Jardins de
Trocadéro
AVENUE D'IÉNA
PONT
D'IÉNA
BRANLY
Esplanade
des
Invalides
**Palais
Bourbon-
Assemblée
Nationale**
**Musée
d'Orsay**
RUE DE BAC
**École des
Beaux Art**

AVE. DU
PRES. KENNEDY
PONT DE
BIR HAKEM
QUAI
Tour Eiffel
AVENUE BOSQUET
7
BLVD. DE LA TOUR-MAUBOURG
RUE ST-GERMAIN
BOULEVAR

Parc du
Champ
de Mars
**Hôtel des
Invalides**
Musée Rodin
BOULEVARD

QUAI DE GRENELLE
BOULEVARD DE GRENELLE
AVE. DE TOURVILLE
BOULEVARD DES INVALIDES
RUE DE RENNES
6

**École
Militaire**
AVE. DE BRETEUIL

AVENUE ÉMILE ZOLA
AVENUE DE LOWENDAL
U.N.E.S.C.O.
BLVD. GARIBALDI
RASPAIL
Jardins
Luxembo

15

RUE LECOURBE
BLVD. PASTEUR
RUE DU MONTPARNASSE

RUE DE VAUGIRARD
**Gare
Montparnasse**
BLVD. DE VAUGIRARD
AVE. DU MAINE
**Tour
Montparnasse**
BLVD. RASPAIL

RUE
LEBLANC
BOULEVARD VICTOR
Cimetière
du
Montparnasse
RUE
FROIDEVAUX

Porte de
Sèvres
Parc des
BOULEVARD LEFEBVRE
AVENUE DU MAINE
AVENUE DE
ROCH

BOULEVARD PERIPHERIQUE
RUE
ERNEST
RENAN
Expositions
Porte de
la Plaine
14
GEN. LECLERC

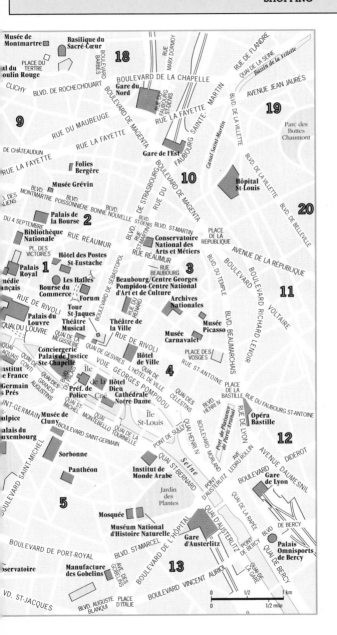

Musée de Montmartre

Basilique du Sacré-Cœur

18

PLACE DU TERTRE

al du oulin Rouge

RUE MARX DORMOY

BOULEVARD BARBÈS

RUE DE FLANDRE

QUAI DE LA SEINE

Bassin de la Villette

CLICHY

BLVD. DE ROCHECHOUART

BOULEVARD DE LA CHAPELLE

Gare du Nord

AVENUE JEAN JAURÈS

19

Parc des Buttes Chaumont

9

RUE DU MAUBEUGE

BOULEVARD DE MAGENTA

RUE LA FAYETTE

RUE DU FAUBOURG ST-DENIS

SAINTE-MARTIN

BLVD. DE LA VILLETTE

DE CHÂTEAUDUN

RUE LA FAYETTE

RUE LA FAYETTE

Gare de l'Est

FAUBOURG

Canal Saint-Martin

Hôpital St-Louis

BLVD. DE LA VILLETTE

Folies Bergère

Musée Grévin

BLVD. MONTMARTRE POISSONNIÈRE

BLVD. DES IENS

BONNE NOUVELLE

BOULEVARD DE STRASBOURG

RUE DU

BOULEVARD DE MAGENTA

10

BLVD. DE BELLEVILLE

20

DU 4 SEPTEMBRE

Palais de la Bourse

2

RUE RÉAUMUR

BLVD. ST-DENIS BLVD. ST-MARTIN

RUE ST-MARTIN

PLACE DE LA RÉPUBLIQUE

Bibliothèque Nationale

PL. DES VICTOIRES

Hôtel des Postes St-Eustache

RUE RÉAUMUR

Conservatoire National des Arts et Métiers

AVENUE DE LA RÉPUBLIQUE

Palais Royal

1

RUE BEAUBOURG

3

BOULEVARD VOLTAIRE

BOULEVARD RICHARD LENOIR

11

médie ançais

Les Halles

Bourse du Commerce

Forum

BOULEVARD DE SÉBASTOPOL

Beaubourg/Centre Georges Pompidou-Centre National d'Art et de Culture

RUE DU TEMPLE

RUE DE RIVOLI

Palais du Louvre

Tour St-Jaques

Théâtre Musical

RUE DU RENARD

Archives Nationales

QUAI DU LOUVRE

QUAI DE LA MÉGISSERIE

Théâtre de la Ville

RUE DE RIVOLI

Musée Picasso

BLVD. BEAUMARCHAIS

QUAI ACQUAIS CONTI

QUAI DES GRANDS AUGUSTINS

Conciergerie Palais de Justice Ste-Chapelle

QUAI DE GESVRES

Musée Carnavalet

Hôtel de Ville

PLACE DES VOSGES

RUE ST-ANTOINE

stitut e France

Île de la Cité

Préf. de Police

Hôtel Dieu

QUAI DE L'HÔTEL DE VILLE

VOIE GEORGES POMPIDOU

4

QUAI DES CÉLESTINS

PLACE DE LA BASTILLE

RUE DU FAUBOURG ST-ANTOINE

Germain e Prés

QUAI ST-MICHEL

Cathédrale Notre Dame

BLVD. HENRI IV

INT-GERMAIN

ulpice

Musée de Cluny

QUAI MONTEBELLO

QUAI DE LA TOURNELLE

Île St-Louis

Opéra Bastille

RUE DE LYON

12

alais du uxembourg

BOULEVARD SAINT-GERMAIN

PONT DE SULLY

QUAI HENRI IV

Port de Plaisance de Paris-Arsenal

AVENUE DAUMESNIL

DIDEROT

Sorbonne

Seine

PONT MORLAND

AVE. LEDRU-ROLLIN

BOULEVARD

Gare de Lyon

BOULEVARD SAINT-MICHEL

Panthéon

Institut de Monde Arabe

QUAI ST-BERNARD

PONT D'AUSTERLITZ

QUAI DE LA RAPÉE

BLVD

DE BERCY

5

Jardin des Plantes

Mosquée

Muséum National d'Histoire Naturelle

Gare d'Austerlitz

QUAI D'AUSTERLITZ

PONT DE BERCY

QUAI DE LA GARE

QUAI DE BERCY

Palais Omnisports de Bercy

BOULEVARD DE PORT-ROYAL

BLVD. ST-MARCEL

RUE DE L'HÔPITAL

bservatoire

Manufacture des Gobelins

AVE. DES GOBELINS

13

BOULEVARD VINCENT AURIOL

VD. ST-JACQUES

BLVD. AUGUSTE BLANQUI

PLACE D'ITALIE

0   1/2   1 km

1/2 mile

are around St-Germain-des-Prés (rue de Sèvres, rue du Cherche-Midi, rue de Grenelle and the place Saint-Sulpice).

The Marais is quieter. New designers show their wares in discreet boutiques under awnings around the place des Victoires (there is even a Kenzo for kids within the main shop) and others. Jean Paul Gaultier has his showpiece in the arcaded *passage* in the rue Vivienne, 2e. There are numerous boutiques in the vast Forum des Halles. The best place of all to shop for clothes is on the designer or own collection floors of Galeries Lafayette or Printemps.

Discounts

Fashion would not be fashion in Paris if it did not date quickly. You can pick up last year's designer labels discounted by up to 50 per cent by shopping in

Hédiard and Fauchon, in the place de la Madeleine, should not be missed by food lovers

the discount shops. Do not expect personal service, changing rooms or to be able to take anything back if you change your mind. Streets to look for include: the rue Saint-Placide, 6e (Moda Soldes sell discounted shoes); the rue Saint-Dominique, 7e (Stock Sacs sell discounted bags). At 65 rue Montmartre, 9e, Mendes sell St Laurent cast-offs. Look for shops with *Stock* in the name (including Cacharel and Dorothée Bis) along the rue d'Alésia, 14e. If you do not mind crowds and are prepared to sort through piles of rubbish, there are also bargains at Tati (branches in: 4–30 boulevard Rochechouart, 18e; at 140 rue de Rennes, 6e and at 13 place de la République, 11e). There is a clothes market in the 3e in the Carreau du Temple.

Fashion shows: If you want to attend a fashion show you need a ticket. Either apply direct to the salon or ask the concierge at your hotel if he can get one for you. The main *haute-couture* collections are in January and July. *Prêt à porter* are in March and October. If you want to find out about any particular designer the Fédération Française de la Couture, du Prêt-à-Porter, des Couturiers et des Createurs de Mode are at 100 rue Faubourg-St-Honoré, 8e. Tel: 42.66.64.44. You can also ask the main fashion houses directly. The Tourist Office has a list of contacts. Both Galeries Lafayette and Printemps hold their own fashion shows. Most are at 11:00 A.M.

Food

If you love food a walk around the place de la Madeleine, 8e will be a mouth-watering experience. Fauchon at number 26 is the jewel in the crown, the world famous *épicier* (grocer) where you can buy everything from fresh *foie gras* to caviar, as well as olive oil, mustards, cheeses and exquisitely prepared dishes to take out from dressed crab to colourful terrines. Upstairs there are biscuits and hundreds of teas, all in attractive tins. Everything at Fauchon is packaged beautifully. Hédiard at no 21 opposite is tiny by comparison but has a wonderful display of exotic fruits under a palm tree. Next to Hédiard is the Maison de la Truffe (no. 19) for fresh truffles,

then comes a little shop that sells nothing but cheese, with a couple of tiny tables neatly laid so you can sample as many as you like. At number 17 the Caviar Kaspia specialises in caviar (you can eat it in the restaurant upstairs), and just in case by this time you are getting thirsty, almost next door there is a branch of the famous L'Ecluse wine bar.

Of course, there are also numerous *charcuteries, fromageries, pâtisseries* all over Paris as well as shops specialising in specific food items from caviar to snails.

For hand-made chocolate try Lenotre, 44 rue de Bac, 7e or 3 rue du Havre, 9e, or the Maison du Chocolat, 225 rue du Faubourg-St-Honoré, 8.

The best ice-cream in Paris is from Berthillon, 31 rue St-Louis-en-L'Ile. Ingenious flavours.

Poilâne, 8 rue du Cherche-Midi, 6e, is possibly the most famous breadshop in France. They specialise in amazing shapes.

At Androuet, 41 rue d'Amsterdam, 8e you can try the famous cheeses (at lunchtime or in the evening) as well as buy regional cheeses in pristine condition from all over France. Flo Prestige, 42 place du Marché-Saint-Honoré, 1er, sells portions of gourmet food.

Gifts, Jewellery and Accessories

Paris is full of exclusive shops selling quality gifts and accessories, although the main stores are much better value. For perfumes all the major houses – Guerlain, Balmain,

Lancôme — have shops, many in the Champs-Elysées, 8e or the place Vendôme, 1er. You will also see shops offering duty-free prices, especially in the avenue de l'Opéra and the Champs-Elysées, but the airport may still be cheaper.

The top jewellers — Boucheron, Cartier, Van Cleef & Arpels — are in the place Vendôme. For luggage, Louis Vuitton in the avenue Marceau, 8e is the top designer. For china and crystal the Lalique shop is at 11 rue Royale in the 8e. Any of the *passages* (see pages 63-64) will yield rewarding shops selling unusual items.

Markets

Paris has over 80 permanent markets, covered and uncovered, offering a range of goods from antiques to food, children's toys to pets. The Mairie de Paris publishes a free list which you can get from the Tourist Office.

Antiques/fleas: For bric à brac and bigger pieces of furniture you can wade through the miles of junk in one of the huge outdoor markets. Be prepared to bargain, get there early and hang onto your valuables. The largest flea market, four miles (six km) long with 3,000 stalls, is the Marché aux Puces (flea market) at the Porte de Clignancourt/Saint Ouen in the 18e (Saturday to Monday). You could also try the Porte de Vanves (avenue Marc Sangnier in the 14e, Saturday and Sunday). For clothes the Porte de Montreuil market in the 20e runs from Saturday to Monday (all day).

Birds: the bird and pet market is held on Sundays in the Marché aux Oiseaux in the place Louis-Lépine on the Ile de la Cité, 4e, where they also sell flowers during the rest of the week. You can also see birds and other animals along the quai de la Mégisserie, 1er.

Clothes: the Carreau du Temple in the Marais, 3e just south of the République is open from 9:00 A.M. to 7:00 P.M. every day except Monday. You can buy antique clothes in the Aligre market, in the place d'Aligre, 12e every morning until 1:00 P.M., except Monday (as well as fruit and vegetables in the neighbouring streets).

Food: There are over 80 food markets in Paris, both uncovered and covered. Among the most lively are: the place Monge, 5e and the streets around the rue Mouffetard; the rue de Buci (6e) and adjoining rue de Seine in the Latin Quarter; Raspail (6e) between the rues du Cherche-Midi et de Rennes; the Charonne near the Bastille in the Ile. Get there early for the still-squirming sea food, the oozing cheeses and the shiny fruit and vegetables that look as if each piece has been individually polished. Buy plaits of garlic and handfuls of herbs to take home or just savour the smells. Buy *saucisson, salami,* or a waxy cardboard box of a divine seafood salad, a piece of cheese, a crisp *baguette,* and a bottle of wine and you have all the ingredients for a wonderful French picnic. Or just take some mouth-watering photos. Most stalls shut up shop at lunchtime and then open again from 4:00 P.M.

*The market in the place
Louis-Lépine on the Ile de la Cité
sells birds and pets on Sundays*

until about 7:30 P.M. Prices are
fixed so do not try to bargain.
Prints: both banks of the River
Seine are lined with *quais*
where prints and second-hand
books are sold. Look for the
quais du Louvre, de la
Mégisserie, 1er, quais des
Grands Augustins, de Conti et
Malaquais in the 6e.
Flowers: the place Louis-Lépine
on the Ile de la Cité (Monday to
Saturday); the place de la
Madeleine, 8e (Tuesday to
Sunday), or the place des
Ternes, 17e (not Monday).

Stamps: the main stamp market
is under the trees between the
avenue Gabriel and the avenue
de Marigny just off the
Champs-Elysées, 8e, Thursdays,
Saturdays and Sundays from
10:00 A.M. to 7:00 P.M.

Les Passages
Paris has nearly 100 *passages,*
glass-domed arcades down which
the early 18th and 19th-century

Parisians could browse without getting wet; the equivalent of the modern shopping mall, with family-run firms selling everything from chops to china. Some have been renovated and now house travel agents, designer boutiques and hairdressers, others are delightfully dilapidated with carved shop fronts, painted ceilings and marble counters. Behind even the most crumbling façades are some of Paris's most interesting shops, many of them family firms going back generations. Most are in the 1er and 2e, although there are others in the 9e and 10e.

The Galerie Vivienne (various entrances, one at 4 rue des Petits Champs, 2e) is one of the most splendid architecturally with wrought-iron work, mosaic tiles and high roof with bas reliefs. Leading off it is the *passage* Colbert where Jean Paul Gaultier has his showroom (complete with fashion shows on videos under glass bubbles on the floor).

The rather grand copper and mahogany fronted Galerie Vero-Dodat built by two butchers in 1824 is at 19 rue Jean-Jacques-Rousseau, 1er. Behind the wooden pillars and gleaming brass doors, there are numerous interesting shops, selling musical instruments, antiques, and antiquarian books. There is also a tiny, intimate restaurant, the Vero Dodat on two floors (closed Sunday and Monday lunch). Also worth a look are the three linked *passages:* des Panoramas, Jouffroy and Verdeau at boulevard Montmartre, 2e.

Shopping Centres

The old Les Halles market is now replaced by the glass and chrome shell of the underground **Forum des Halles**, 1–7 rue Pierre-Lescot, 1er. It is the largest pedestrian shopping area in Europe, with four levels of shops, discos, banks, restaurants and cinemas reached by escalators. The place is full of boutiques and designer furniture shops, art galleries and cafés. If you need to cool off in a hurry, there is an indoor swimming pool at the Nouveau Forum opposite the church of St-Eustache.

The Palais des Congrès shopping centre (2 place de la Porte Maillot, 17e) is inside the convention building: a vast complex with shops, restaurants, cinemas and an air terminal. The huge Concorde-Lafayette Hotel (almost 1,000 rooms) is also part of the complex.

The Montparnasse-Maine Centre, 15e, between the rue de L'Arrivée and the rue du Départ (next to the Air France terminal), is now the heart of the business area of Paris, dominated by the 686ft (209m) Maine Montparnasse Tower, which has one of the best views of the city from the observatory on the 56th floor. The commercial/shopping centre is on eight levels, six of them underground with the upper three floors devoted to fashion shops, restaurants and cafés (including a branch of Galeries Lafayette). The rest includes a vast parking lot and a sports centre with public swimming pool.

FOOD AND DRINK

Eating Out

Do not assume that just because you are in Paris wherever you eat the food will be good, nor will it even necessarily be French. The city is full of mediocre restaurants of every nationality, as well as some of the very best restaurants in the world. And the good ones are not always expensive. Although you can get in line at one of the many brasseries in the capital, or take your chances at one of the many cheap bistros, the very best restaurants (and not necessarily the most expensive) get booked up and

Whenever possible Parisians sit out in the open air, especially on the Left Bank around St-Michel

need reserving well in advance. What you might find disappointing if you are planning a short visit to the city is that many of these restaurants close on weekends. And if you are visiting in July or August they may well be shut for the entire month for their vacations. Many restaurants serve a fixed price menu for a number of francs (especially at lunchtime), which can even make the most expensive restaurants in Paris manageable. This might include three or four courses, with a number of choices within each. Wine is also sometimes included. Service and tax are always included so there is no need to leave a tip. Lunchtime is always busy in a good Parisian restaurant. They eat early with

FOOD AND DRINK

last orders well before 2:30 P.M. but then if you want a drink and a snack mid-afternoon you can go to a café or *salon de thé*. In the evening last orders in some restaurants may be 9:30 or 10:00 P.M. Many brasseries open until 1 or 2 in the morning and most are open at weekends. Your best guide to where to get the best food is the red *Michelin* Guide to Paris or the *Gault Millau* to France, a bible of a book, which describes restaurants in detail, though unfortunately only in French. For cheap restaurants, *Paupers' Paris* by Miles Turner (Pan) has a good selection. I have picked out a selection of restaurants in different categories in central areas:

Brasseries
Brasseries tend to be big, noisy and bustling. The food is usually good, many brasseries have displays of seafood outside, and also serve Alsatian specialities like sauerkraut. The service is fast, and the clientele mixed. Many serve meals after midnight and are open every day. Because of their size you are more likely to get a table without a reservation though you will probably have to wait. The following are among those with the best food and/or the most character:

Bofinger, 5 rue de la Bastille, 4e (tel: 42.72.87.82). Near the new Opera house, very popular and open every day until 1:00 A.M. One of the very first brasseries, with ornate Belle Epoque decor and gilt mirrors, seats 300 in several different areas. They serve vast platters of seafood,

excellent *bouillabaisse* and Alsatian specialities.

Le Boeuf sur le Toit, 34 rue du Colisée, 8e (tel: 43.59.83.80). Art Deco and Art Nouveau decor, seafood on display in the outer courtyard. Fashionable. Good reasonably priced food. Open daily until 2:00 A.M.

Brasserie Flo, 7 cour des Petites-Ecuries, 10e (tel: 47.70.13.59). Wonderful display of still squirming seafood outside, turn-of-the-century decor inside. Worth the trip to get there and the line to get in. Open every day until 1:30 A.M.

Brasserie Lipp, 151 boulevard St-Germain, 6e (tel: 45.48.53.91). Opposite the famous cafés de Flore and Deux Magots. Up-scale meeting place. Good food, serious meals rather than snacks. On two floors. They turn away people they do not like the look of and put doubtfuls on the first floor. Open until 1:00 A.M. Not cheap. Closed on Mondays.

Brasserie Saint-Benoît, 26 rue Saint-Benoît, 6e (tel: 45.48.29.66). Very cheap traditional brasserie in St-Germain, especially if you stick to the set menus. Outside terrace. Closed Sunday. Open until midnight.

Chez Jenny, 39 Boulevard du Temple, 3e. (tel: 42.74.75.75). Popular brasserie serving Alsatian food of the *choucroute* variety as well as substantial French dishes. Seats 625 in five separate rooms. Still going strong after 30 years. Open every day until 1:00 A.M.

La Coupole, 102 boulevard du Montparnasse, 14e (tel: 43.20.14.20). One of Paris' best-known and loved brasseries,

FOOD AND DRINK

*Brasseries serve the best seafood —
this one is the Terminus Nord*

newly renovated. An enormous
1930s-style meeting place (with
a ballroom for tea dances downstairs) once popular with intellectuals. Run by the people who
own Brasserie Flo, Chez Julien
and Terminus Nord. Open until
2:00 A.M. Combine with a climb
up the Montparnasse Tower.
Terminus Nord, 23 rue de
Dunkerque, 10e (tel: 42.85.05.15).
Opposite the station (there are
two, this is the one with a
display of seafood outside). If
you have just come in by train,
an excellent place to get
acclimatised. Excellent food
(also drinks *only*). A good taste
of things to come. Open every
day until 12:30 A.M.
Vaudeville, 29 rue Vivienne, 2e
(tel: 42.33.39.31). Open until 2:00
A.M. every day. Near the Bourse,
so popular with city slickers at
lunchtime. 1920s decor. Good

seafood, lively and reasonably
priced.

Drugstores
Drugstores do not sell drugs (at
least not openly) but drinks,
meals, books, clothes and
souvenirs. They tend to open
until late, and attract
disorientated visitors and Paris
youngsters. An inexpensive
place to eat steak, ice-cream
and hamburgers. One of the
most popular is at the top of the
Champs-Elysées, **Publicis
Champs-Elysées** at no. 133.
There is another, the **Publis
Saint-Germain,** next to Brasserie
Lipp at 149 boulevard
St-Germain. They are good
places to arrange to meet
someone, to use the phone,
restroom etc. Others include:
Le Drugstorian, 1 avenue
Matignon, 8e
New Store, 63 Champs-
Elysées, 8e
Pub Renault, 53 Champs-
Elysées, 8e

FOOD AND DRINK

Ethnic Food/Snacks and Take-Out *(casse-croute)*

Most of the department stores have reasonably priced snack bars and restaurants, as do many of the museums. Some snack bars, especially those selling ethnic food may be open 24 hours. If you have no time to sit down, you can buy a *crêpe* from one of the *crêperie* stands, a thin pancake made in front of you on a flat, black iron ring and stuffed full of jam or other concoctions. You could also try a *crôque monsieur* (toasted ham and cheese sandwich) or a *crôque madame* (toasted cheese and ham with a fried egg), plus various varieties of *sandwich*.

Charcuteries/traiteurs are a good source of snacks; they will usually stuff a *baguette* full of salami and sell wonderful salads in waxy containers for you to take away. A plastic knife and fork will come in handy as they are sometimes not supplied and you could have a messy grapple with the ingredients. Cafés and *salons de thé* serve snacks. You may see an *assiette anglaise* on the menu (plate of mixed cold meats). Most places serve omelettes.

There is a concentration of ethnic take-outs in the Latin Quarter in the rue Huchette, 5e and in the rue Mouffetard among others. The stalls sell

Jo Goldenberg's restaurant and delicatessen in the Marais

Moroccan, Greek, Middle Eastern, Italian, American and French specialities. You can get Russian take-out in the Marais or, if your imagination runs no further there are branches of McDonald's and a Burger King in the Champs-Elysées.
Ethnic restaurants include:
Japanese: Le Yamato in the Hôtel Meridien (81 boulevard Gouvion-St-Cyr, 17e) and **Nikko** (61 quai Grenelle, 15e) both have excellent Japanese restaurants.
Jewish: Jo Goldenberg's, 7 rue des Rosiers, 4e, (tel: 48.87.20.16), serves everything from chicken soup to chopped liver, plus a take-out deli bar. Open on Saturdays. Also at 69 avenue Wagram, 17e.
Mexican: the trendy **Café Pacifico,** 50 boulevard Montparnasse, 15e (tel: 45.48.63.87), serves a Mexican brunch, with band, on a Sunday.
North African: Trois Horloges, 73 rue Brancion, 15e (tel: 48.28.24.08), *bouillabaisse, couscous* and other Franco/Algerian specialities. Closed Tuesday lunch and Monday.
Russian: Dominique, 19 rue Bréa, 6e (tel: 43.27.08.80). Borscht and caviar either to take away or eat there. Reasonable prices. Or try the fashionable **La Tchaika** (closed Sundays), 7 rue de Lappe, 11e near the Bastille (tel: 47.00.73.61) or **Datcha Lydie,** 7 rue Dupleix, 15e (tel: 45.66.67.77). Closed Wednesday.
Vietnamese: Tan Dinh, 60 rue de Verneuil, 7e (tel: 45.44.04.84).

Highly rated restaurant serving sophisticated Vietnamese cuisine. Closed Sunday.
If you cannot make up your mind which nationality you want to sample, the **Savannah Café**, 27 rue Descartes, 5e (tel: 43.29.45.77) offers food from around the world. Otherwise there are Korean, Indian, Brazilian, Italian, Scandinavian, Turkish, Dutch, American and English possibilities . . . The English language *Passion* magazine (published every two months) lists many of them and the red *Michelin* guide singles out the best.

French Restaurants – Cheap
You will see *Les Selfs,* or self-service restaurants, all over the city. You do not need to speak the language as the food is displayed on counters and there are special daily dishes to choose from. Cheap, cheerful and quick once you get past the lunchtime lines. Several of the department stores have self-service restaurants including Monoprix in the avenue de l'Opéra, 1er, Printemps, which offers counters of food of various nationalities under the stained-glass dome and Galeries Lafayette in boulevard Haussmann. From the roof terrace on the 10th floor of Magasin 2 of La Samaritaine in the rue de la Monnaie there are good views. You can also buy snacks in galleries and museums. Few cheap restaurants take reservations, so turn up early or be prepared to wait.

FOOD AND DRINK

Here is a short selection of restaurants if you are on a tight budget.

Chartier, 7 rue du Faubourg Montmartre, 9e. Revolving doors lead to huge soup kitchen with 1920s decor, mirrors, shared tables and lines for the food which is excellent value. Closes at 9:30 P.M. Open every day.

Le Drouet, 103 rue de Richelieu, 2e. Owned by the same people as Chartier and similar. Open every day. Near the large department stores and the Opéra.

Restaurant du Grand Cerf, passage du Grand Cerf, 2e (off the rue Saint-Denis). Noisy, busy and very cheap serving Spanish and French dishes up until 9:30 P.M.

La Canaille, 4 rue Crillon, 4e. Near the port by the Bastille. Popular with students. Closed weekends.

Le Polidor, 41 rue Monsieur-le-Prince, 6e. Famous cheap restaurant, some 50 years old with good food and shared tables. James Joyce used to like it.

Le Trumilou, 84 quai de l'Hôtel-de-Ville, 4e. Small, bright, unpretentious, hundred-year-old restaurant and bar, fresh flowers and pretty crockery. Very cheap set menus, views of Notre-Dame. Closed Mondays.

French Restaurants – Reasonable

Prices soon add up if you order *à la carte,* but stick to the set menu and the house wine (carafe) in some of the places listed below and your bill

should still be considerably less than the equivalent meal in London or New York.

Ambassade d'Auvergne, 22 rue du Grenier St-Lazare, 3e. (tel: 42.72.31.22). Fashionable, long-established restaurant near Les Halles, serving somewhat hearty regional recipes of the Auvergne. Plats de Saison good value. Open every day.

La Cagouille, 10 place Brancusi, 14e. (tel: 43.22.09.01). Well-known for its fish and excellent value. Near the Montparnasse Tower. Noted for its collection of Cognacs and food from the same region. Closed Sunday and Monday.,

Chez Quinson, 5 place Etienne-Pernet, 15e. (tel: 45.32.48.54). Not right in the centre but worth a visit if you like *bouillabaisse* and food from Provence. Closed Sunday and Monday. Last orders 9:30 P.M.

FOOD AND DRINK

The temptations of a pâtisserie . . .

Dodin-Bouffant, 25 rue Frédéric Sauton, 5e. (tel: 43.25.25.14). Big, popular, old-fashioned, unpretentious place on two floors with more atmosphere downstairs than up. Hearty portions. Well-known for its raspberry soufflé. Good value for the money. Closed Sunday in August.

Chez Pauline, 5 rue Villedo, 1er (tel: 42.96.20.70). Highly rated intimate restaurant on two floors, serving classical French cuisine in a formal setting. Closed Saturday evening and Sunday.

Au Pied de Cochon, 6 rue Coquillière, 1er (tel: 42.36.11.75). Famous old Les Halles restaurant that used to be packed with market traders. Open all day and night for dishes like onion soup, oysters and pig's feet.

Le Pharamond, 24 rue de la Grande-Truanderie, 1er. (tel: 42.33.06.72). Closed Monday lunch and Sunday, end of July to end of August. Famous turn of the century restaurant of Les Halles, serving *tripes à la mode de Caen.*

Le Récamier, 4 rue Récamier, 7e (tel: 45.48.86.58). Intimate, first-class food. Closed Sunday.

French Restaurants — Expensive

You can spend a fortune in one of the best restaurants in Paris but the sumptuous settings of some of these restaurants are almost worth paying for in themselves. The following are among the very best, regularly scooping Michelin rosettes.

Les Ambassadeurs, Hotel de Crillon, 10 place de la Concorde, 8e. (tel: 42.65.24.24). One of the most sumptuous dining rooms in Paris. Palatial 18th-century decor, chandeliers, mirrors and marble, plus terrace overlooking the place de la Concorde. Outstanding kitchen with simple dishes as well as elaborate ones.

L'Ambroisie, 9 place des Vosges, 4e (tel: 42.78.51.45). Tiny, sophisticated restaurant with superb cooking, in an old silversmith's shop under the arcades in the heart of the Marais. Closed Sunday and Monday lunchtime.

Jamin, 32 rue de Longchamp, 16e. (tel: 47.27.12.27). Small restaurant well-known for the creativity and inventiveness of its highly acclaimed chef. Modern French cuisine using the very best ingredients from all over France. The fixed

FOOD AND DRINK

priced menu is excellent value.
Closed Saturday and Sunday.
La Jules Verne, 2nd floor, south pillar, Eiffel Tower, 7e. (tel: 45.55.61.44). Wonderful views, and surprisingly good food. Has its own private elevator. Attracts business people and birthday parties. Piano bar, but only with reservations, after 10:30 at night.
Lucas-Carton, place 9 de la Madeleine, 8e (tel: 42.65.22.90). Old-established and very expensive top restaurant with art nouveau decor. Closed Saturday and Sunday.
Taillevent, 15 rue Lamennais, 8e. (tel: 45.63.39.34). Another outstanding restaurant, some rate it the best in Paris, so much so that tables have to be reserved months in advance. Spacious, mansion-like restaurant with a club-like atmosphere, wood-panelled rooms and crystal chandeliers. Closed Saturday and Sunday.

Where to drink

Bars and Cafés
Paris is crammed full of bars and cafés: dingy, smoky, deafeningly noisy bars where everyone stands at a narrow chrome counter; bars with pinball machines and adjacent restaurants; trendy basement bars with potted plants, designer furniture and jazz musicians; old fashioned piano bars in top hotels like the de Crillon; book shop bars; museum and art gallery bars and, of course, the famous bars on the Left Bank, the regular watering-holes of intellectuals from Sartre to Hemingway.
The first thing you should know is that it is cheaper to stand up at the bar than to sit down at a table, where a service charge will be added to your bill. Also, that bars on the main boulevards

The Café de Flore, as popular with Parisians as visitors, was patronised by Picasso

(Champs-Elysées, Rivoli, Faubourg-St-Honoré, St-Germain and St-Michel among them), as well as in places like the Beaubourg, around the Opéra and in the main squares, charge a lot more for their drinks than those in side streets round the corner. You can sit outside, or under a glass roof, at those typical round tables that are barely big enough for the drinks, and people-watch. Almost all bars serve snacks of some kind. If you are a beer drinker and want to save money, ask for *une demi* or *pression*, otherwise you will get a large glass or the more expensive bottled variety. Beer is cheaper than mineral water. Many bars stay open until 2:00 A.M.

Paris also has its fair share of English-style pubs and American cocktail bars and wine bars where wine is taken seriously and sold by the glass.

The following bars and cafés are among the most famous (and some of the most expensive) in the city.

Café Costes, 4 rue Berger, 1er. Very trendy, noisy, crowded and stylish. A modern version of the Grand Café designed to last 100 years! Open until 2:00 A.M.

Café Beaubourg, 45 rue St-Merri, 4e. Similar style to the Café Costes but less frenetic. Open until 2:00 A.M.

Café de Flore, 172 boulevard St-Germain, 6e. A Left Bank café/brasserie much loved by Picasso, Camus and Simone de Beauvoir. You can sit outside. Open every day until 1:30 A.M.

L'Entre-Pôts, 14 rue de Charonne, 11e. Heart of the Bastille nightlife area. Sophisticated bar with cool modern decor and exotic cocktails.

Harry's Bar, 5 rue Daunou, 2e. An American bar where they have been mixing drinks for people like Hemingway since 1921. Exotic cocktails and piano bar in the basement. Open until 4:00 A.M.

La Coupole, 102 boulevard du Montparnasse, 14e. Huge *brasserie* and American bar, newly re-vamped, popular with intellectuals past and present.

Hôtel de Crillon, 10 place de la Concorde, 8e. Plush, elegant setting, in a former palace, with pianist.

Le Grand Café, 4 boulevard des Capucines, 9e. Very grand large restaurant/café near the Opéra, in the Belle Epoque style, open day and all night.

Aux Deux Magots, 170 boulevard St-Germain, 6e. The famous café where Sartre watched the girls go by for inspiration. Still a meeting place with tables spilling out onto the pavement and views of St-Germain-des-Prés.Try the hot chocolate or the numerous brands of whisky. Also a brasserie. Open until 2:00 A.M. every day.

Lipp, 151 boulevard St-Germain, 6e. Opposite Flore and Aux Deux Magots, making up the famous threesome. More of a brasserie than a café.

Salons de Thé (tea shops)

There are plenty of tea shops in Paris, some grand, some tiny. Most of them open from noon until early evening and serve light meals, irresistible cakes and ice-creams. Some are in *pâtisseries*. **Fauchon**, for

FOOD AND DRINK

Fanny's tiny tea shop, between the Pont Neuf and the Conciergerie in the place Dauphine

example, at 26 place de la Madeleine, 8e, serve their irresistible cakes at narrow chrome counters.

One of the most famous and oldest (1903) *salons de thé* is **Angelina's** in the rue de Rivoli, 1er (no. 226) near the Louvre, well-known for their hot chocolate with whipped cream, as is **Laduree's** tea room and *pâtisserie* (16 rue Royale, 8e), an opulant *salon de thé* with Louis XIV decor where they make their own chocolates.

On the Ile de la Cité (4e) you can have a real English tea at **Fanny's**, 20 place Dauphine, a tiny old-fashioned, homely place.

There are several tea shops in splendid settings, including: **La Pagode** (52 bis rue de Babylone, 7e), an original Japanese pagoda, now a cinema. You can have tea in the garden whether you see a film or not. The Moroccan **Café de la Mosquée** (rue Geoffroy-St-Hilaire, 5e), near the Jardin des Plantes, serves mint tea in the mosque itself and on a patio in the garden when the weather is fine. In the Marais, at 37 rue Vieille du Temple, you can have tea upstairs at **Christhiey Paris** in among an eccentric tropical jungle of buddhas, plants and furniture. A pianist plays downstairs. You can also have an English tea in **W H Smith's Bookshop** at 248 rue de Rivoli. The best ice-cream in Paris is from **Berthillon's** at 31, rue St-Louis-en L'Ile, 4e.

Wine Bars

Wine bars are expensive and take their wines seriously. A glass can cost as much as a bottle in a brasserie. Although you do not usually go to eat, they also serve simple dishes — perhaps some salami or cheese or a slice of *foie gras*. The Paris wine bar scene more or less began with the British owned **Willi's** (13 rue des Petits-Champs, 1er), which also serves light meals; the **Blue Fox** (25 rue de Royale, 8e) and **Le Petit Bacchus** (13 rue du Cherche-Midi, 6e). All are trendy watering-holes and the staff speaks English so you will get good advice on what to drink. Look for bars in the **L'Ecluse** chain. Many wine bars close on weekends.

FOOD AND DRINK

Cheese and Wine

Virtually everyone spending time in Paris is going to want to sample the wine; after all, it's one of the best things about France! A good deal of nonsense is talked about wine, and that tends to cloud the fact that drinking it is a pleasure, and a pleasure that can become more and more fascinating as you discover the subtleties of different kinds. So, try a variety, and why not try them with some of the speciality cheeses of the area around Paris?

Cheese

France is the largest producer of cheese in the world after the USA, with each region producing its own speciality. The Ile de France, the area around Paris, produces a number of cheeses of which the most famous is the brie de Meaux, round and flat and covered in a white mould, voted 'King of Cheeses' in 1815 by the 143 negotiators of the Congress of Vienna. But brie dates back even further than that. In the 15th century, Charles d'Orléans, father of Louis XII, used to order bries by the dozen to give as New Year presents. There are many different varieties, but when you are choosing any of them look for a round cheese that bulges, rather than runs, when you press it. It should be pale yellow with a reddish crust streaked with white.

The Ile de France is also known for its rich soft creamy cheeses. If you want to sample something relatively local try:

Boursin: famous soft cheese flavoured with herbs and garlic with a high fat content. Also exported and made in Normandy.

Brie de Coulommiers: a rich sharp cheese, often used in cooking. Sometimes with added cream. Not the same as the commercially produced coulommier.

Brie laitier: a commercially produced pasteurised cheese.

A tempting display of cheeses, typical of any delicatessen

FOOD AND DRINK

Brie de Meaux fermier: the King of Cheeses. Look for a white crust, slightly marked with red or brown. The inside is pale yellow and slightly firm.

Brie de Melun: reputed to be even older than the Meaux. Made from raw cow's milk and produced in small dairies in the traditional manner. A bit smellier than the Meaux and generally squatter and thicker.

Brie de Montereau: Also known as Ville St-Jacques. A bit like a camembert but with a fruitier flavour.

Chèvru: an upmarket cheese a bit like a Meaux. Made on a farm and also known as fougère or fougèru.

Coulommiers: a smaller version of the Meaux. Sold commercially when the straw it is supposed to mature on is often plastic. A creamy cheese with a white crust.

Délice de St-Cyr: a rich creamy cheese to eat with a fruity wine. Triple cream cheese with a mild flavour.

Explorateur: the commercial variety of a triple cream cheese.

Feuille de Dreux: when they made it at home it was wrapped in chestnut leaves. Low-fat cheese made from partially

The food markets are always lively and are excellent places to buy all kinds of cheeses

skimmed milk with a strong flavour.

Fontainebleau: fresh, rich, creamy dessert cheese made with whipped cream. Eaten with sugar, cold.

Ville St-Jacques: another name for the brie de Montereau.

Wines

What to look for

AC or AOC: *Apellation contrôlée* on a label means you should be getting a decent wine with a guarantee of origin, of production method and of grape variety used. The quantity produced is also controlled. This is not always enough to tell you if the wine is particularly good. Good Bordeaux wines, for example, are also recognised by the name of the château they come from.

VDQS: Vins Délimités de Qualité Superieure denotes a wine produced to encourage the improvement of mediocre wines (many of them from the south of France).

Vins du pays: good value or sometimes better, made from specified variety of grape from the area indicated on the bottle.

Vin de table: may be made from a mixture of grape types or a blend, not even necessarily from France.

Wines with your cheese

There are no rules when it comes to choosing a wine to drink with your cheese. Any strong cheese will completely obscure the flavour of the wine anyway. Choose a good quality wine only if your cheese is mild and in the best possible condition. To be general and

A quality wine is recognised by the name of its château (estate)

safe, try a red Bordeaux for a strong cheese, a white Bordeaux or Burgundy for a creamy one, or a glass of cold champagne.

As a rough guide:
Blue veined cheeses *(bleu de Bresse)* need a young red wine like a Moulin à Vent, a sweet white, or even port.

Creamy cheeses (brie or camembert) go with most wines, especially if their flavour is on the mild side.

Goat cheeses *(chèvre)* need a white with a strong flavour like a Sancerre or a sweet wine like a Sauternes.

Wines to take home

You should know what you want before you start shopping for wine to take home — there is more to a wine than just the label. It is always worth looking for the special offers in the supermarkets (Monoprix) where even the ordinary prices are

FOOD AND DRINK

usually well below those of the winemerchants.
Well worth investing in are liqueurs like the blackcurrant-flavoured **cassis** to use with white wine to make Kir. You can also buy unflavoured **eaux de vie** to preserve fruit, or flavoured varieties to drink as a liqueur, like pear or raspberry.

The label on the bottle will tell you a certain amount about the quality of the wine — but the only way to discover its own particular flavour and aroma is to try a glassful. Below: a wine-tasting

ACCOMMODATION

There are hotels of every sort in Paris. Depending on your budget you will not be stuck for choice, though you may be for a vacancy if you arrive in the middle of a large trade fair or exhibition. You cannot go far wrong if you choose from the red *Michelin* guide (they publish a slim booklet solely on Paris). But pick your area carefully (see The Different Areas pages 11-20). You can get a free booklet listing a selection of Paris hotels from the Tourist Office who will also help you find a room, for a small fee. The busiest times of year are June, September and October, and a useful leaflet, *Choose the Best Period For Your Stay*, is available from the tourist office.

Eating in hotels

Customary waking-up noises in Paris are the clatter of garbage can lids and the whine of street-cleaning trucks, church bells,

Breakfast at the Crillon

shop shutters being rolled up and police car sirens. Pull open your own shutters and you may be able to smell newly baked croissants and strong coffee, although the aromas may not be coming from your own hotel. Although you can get breakfast in all hotels, in cheaper hotels it may be better to go down the road to a nearby bar rather than face slow service, stale rolls, cartons of sterilised milk and undrinkable coffee.

Only the relatively expensive hotels have full restaurants. Unless your hotel is well-known for its restaurant, it is better to eat out. See pages 65-74.

B&B/Efficiencies

The tourist office issues a guide, *Residences de Tourisme*, which lists star-rated apartments. But you can also rent an apartment or stay with a Parisian family through the Chambres chez l'habitant et appartements équipés organisation. Contact them at 73 rue Notre-Dame des Champs, 6e. Tel: 43.25.43.97.

Café-Couette is a network of
private families who wish to
meet overseas guests and
welcome them like friends into
their own homes. They publish a
list of host members all over
France.

Hotels
Expensive
The most exclusive and
expensive hotels are in the 8e
and the 1er *arrondissements*.
One of the only luxury hotels still
in French hands is the
18th-century **de Crillon** (tel:
42.65.24.24) a former palace on
the place de la Concorde, with
elegant yet intimate salons and
sumptuous marble restaurant,
Les Ambassadeurs (where you

*The lavishly decorated Crillon hotel,
an 18th-century palace*

can also have breakfast). Others
include the opulent
Plaza-Athénée in among the
haute couture salons of the
avenue Montaigne, 8e (tel:
47.23.78.33); the **Ritz** in the place
Vendôme, 1er, with its splendid
Louis XV salons and rococo
bedrooms (tel: 42.60.38.30). It
has a splendid new health club,
complete with all the most
modern facilities and fads,
including underwater music in
the marble pool. The grand
Bristol (tel: 42.66.91.45) in the
Faubourg-St-Honoré, 8e has
Gobelin tapestries, old masters
and a swimming pool; and the

The peaceful courtyard of the exclusive Lancaster Hotel

small, refined and elegantly old fashioned **Lancaster** (tel: 43.59.90.43) with a pretty courtyard in the relatively quiet rue de Berri off the Champs-Elysées, 8e.
Do not be afraid to enter the foyers of these luxury hotels, to sit down and take the weight off your feet. You are unlikely to be turned away; look as if you are a customer and enjoy the comings and goings of those who are. The Left Bank has fewer luxury hotels. One of them is the tiny **L'Hôtel Guy-Louis-Duboucheron** (tel: 43.25.27.22) at 13 rue des Beaux-Arts in St-Germain-des-Prés, 6e, where Oscar Wilde died. The decor is mildly eccentric and it has a popular tropical winter garden and piano bar. On the Right Bank, the 7e offers the **Pont Royal** (tel: 45.44.38.27) and the **Sofitel** (tel: 45.55.91.80). In the respectable part of the 9e, you will find the **Grand Hotel Intercontinental** 2 rue Scribe (tel: 42.68.12.13) with its famous restaurant the Opéra-Café de la Paix, and the **Scribe** in the same street (tel: 47.42.03.40). Further out in the 11e arrondissement is the **Holiday Inn** (tel: 43.55.44.34) in the place de la République. Business people tend to stay at the **Méridien Montparnasse**

ACCOMMODATION

(tel: 43.20.15.51) or the **Pullman
Saint-Jaques** (tel: 40.78.79.80) in
the 14e. Alternatively, the **Hilton**
(tel: 42.73.92.00), the **Sofitel** (tel:
40.60.30.30) with its indoor pool,
or the ultra modern **Nikko de
Paris** (tel: 40.58.20.00) are in
the 15e.

The **Citodel Park Avenue et
Central Park** (tel: 45.53.44.60)
and the elegant Louis XVI-
style **Raphaël** (tel: 45.02.16.00)
near the Arc de Triomphe are
in the fashionable residential
16e. In the 17e you will find
the huge, modern 1,000-roomed
Concorde Lafayette (tel:
40.68.50.68) at Montparnasse,
which has splendid views
from the bar on the 34th floor
and the even bigger, over-
1,000-roomed **Méridien Paris
Etoile** (tel: 40.68.34.34) which is
well-known for its jazz.

Reasonable

There are, of course, plenty of
other, less expensive
possibilities. Hundreds of
three-star hotels offer varying
degrees of service and comfort.
To pick out just a few of the
more central hotels:
On the Left Bank you could not
choose a better location than
the rue Jacob in St-Germain-
des-Prés, 6e. There are several
excellent hotels in this street
including no 44 where
Hemingway lived, now the
Angleterre (tel: 42.60.34.72) with
its conservatory-style garden;
Des Deux Continents (tel:
43.26.72.46); the **Danube** (tel:
42.60.94.07), and the quiet **des
Marronniers** (tel: 43.25.30.60),
with antiques and old wooden
beams.
On the Right Bank, on the Île

*The 400-year-old Henri IV hotel, one
of the cheapest in the capital, in the
place Dauphine*

St Louis, 4e, the sister hotels
Deux Iles (tel: 43.26.13.35) and
Lutèce (tel: 43.26.23.52) are also

quiet retreats converted out of 17th-century houses. Equally historic is the **Bretonnerie** (tel: 48.87.77.63) in rue Ste-Croix-de-la-Bretonnerie across the Seine in the Marais (in the street where gay Paris

tends to congregate).

In the 1er the Regency style **Des Tuileries** (tel: 42.61.04.17) is in the rue Saint-Hyacinthe near the place Vendôme and in the same area Paris's oldest hotel the **Molière** (tel: 42.96.22.01), once used as a theatre, is in the rue de Molière.

In the 8e the **Bradford** (tel: 43.59.24.20) in rue St-Philippe-du-Roule is one of the most reasonably priced hotels near the Champs-Elysées. Also very central is the **Résidence La Concorde** (tel: 42.60.38.89) in the rue de Cambon 1er, almost opposite the Tuileries, a good example of a Tradotel, a group of around 100 hotels in central Paris in traditional buildings of character, completely modernised to three-star standards (tel: 47.27.15.15).

Cheap

At the lower end of the market there are plenty of decent two-star hotels and surprisingly acceptable one-stars. You may not get a lounge area, private bathroom, bar or restaurant and it could be a steep hike up to the fifth floor without an elevator. While some cheaper hotels are little gems, tucked away in quiet side streets (or at least with rooms overlooking quiet courtyards), others are drab, noisy and grimy. You may be kept awake by noisy plumbing, creaking beds from the room next door, flickering neon lights or traffic. Although there are plenty of cheap hotels in desirable areas, like the 6e, 5e, or 4e, be careful of those around the Gare du Nord (10e) or Pigalle (9e). As

ACCOMMODATION

well as being noisy you may also find that your hotel is being used for less desirable activities and women who do not want to be pestered may prefer to choose a more salubrious area.

The following are cheap, comfortable and central:

On the Left Bank in the 6e, the **Welcome** (tel: 46.34.24.80) in the rue de Seine right on top of the food market, the 17th-century **Résidence de Globe** (tel: 43.26.35.50) in the rue des Quatre-Vents with its antiques and old beams and the **Récamier** (tel: 43.26.04.89) in the place St-Sulpice, quiet but very central, opposite the church of St-Germain-des-Prés.

In the 5e there is the 17th-century **Esmeralda** (tel: 43.54.19.20),on six floors with no elevator, old-fashioned but with a lot of character, at 4 rue St-Julien-le-Pauvre near Notre-Dame. Or the **Grands Écoles** (tel. 43.26.79.23) at 75 rue du Cardinal-Lemoine, not grand at all but a comfortable country house with garden.

Across the Seine, you could try the modern **Ducs de Bourgogne** (tel: 42.33.95.64) at 19 rue du Pont Neuf 1er or the **Hotel Family** (tel: 42.61.54.84) at 35 rue Cambon 1er. On the Ile de la Cité the **Henry IV** (tel: 43.54.44.53) in a 400-year-old building overlooks the quiet place Dauphine. It is fairly basic, but very cheap.

In the Marais you will find relative peace in the **Hotel Places des Vosges** (tel: 42.72.60.46) at 12 rue de Birague, 4e and at the **Vieux Marais** (tel: 42.78.47.22) at 8 rue du Plâtre, 4e.

Youth Hostels

The Acceuil des Jeunes en France (AJF) have 8,000 beds all year round and 11,000 available in the summer, when they use the Cité University. The head office is at 12 rue des Barres, 4e (tel: 42.72.72.09), or you can visit them at the Gare du Nord arrival hall (March to November); opposite the Pompidou Centre at 119 rue St-Martin, 4e (open all year); at the Hôtel-de-Ville at 16 rue du Pont-Louis-Philippe 4e (June to September); or in the 5e in the Latin Quarter at 139 boulevard St-Michel (March to October). The offices also offer an information service, meal vouchers, student restaurants and reduced cost train and bus tickets. In summer the office at the Gare du Nord is open seven days a week from 8:00 A.M. to 10:00 P.M. The other offices (except the one opposite the Pompidou Centre which is open on Saturday) are only open from Monday to Friday.

With international Youth Hostel Association membership you can reserve a place with a deposit of 50F:

> Auberge de Jeunesse Jules Ferry, 8 boulevard Jules Ferry, Paris 75011
> tel: 43.57.55.60
> Auberge de Jeunesse D'Artagnan, 80 rue Vitruve, Paris 75020 tel: 43.61.08.75

The bureaux d'acceuil run by the Tourist Board (office at the top of the Champs-Elysées open every day, offices at main stations, closed Sundays) also have cheap accommodation on their books.

PARIS BY NIGHT

There are endless night-time possibilities in Paris, from sleazy jazz clubs to glamorous cabarets. There is no one specific area for nightlife, although different activities tend to concentrate themselves into one area. If you want to head for a concentration of lively streets and after-dark activities try:

THE LEFT BANK

The streets around St-Germain-des-Prés (6e) are full of late night bars, cafés and jazz clubs. The rue de la Huchette has many ethnic restaurants and a good jazz club, and the boulevard

See the lights by bâteau mouche

Saint-Michel is always packed until the small hours. The boulevard Montparnasse and the rue de la Gaîté in the 14e offer discos and sex shows although on a much smaller scale than, for example, Pigalle.

THE RIGHT BANK

The Red Light district is Pigalle (9e and 18e) around the boulevard Clichy (see Sex Shows, page 92). The streets around the Forum des Halles, going towards Châtelet are lively late at night. The partly pedestrian-only rue des Lombards is full of jazz clubs; the sex shows are in

PARIS BY NIGHT

The can-can girls at the Moulin Rouge — familiar to many from Toulouse-Lautrec's posters — are still kicking, 100 years on

the rue St-Denis. In the Marais (4e), you will find discreet clubs and discos in the rue Vieille du Temple, and a concentration of gay bars in the rue Ste-Croix-de-la-Bretonnerie. The Bastille (11e) has a few strip clubs and sleazy dives, plus trendy bars and nightclubs with live music plus an old-time musical hall, all concentrated in a low-key triangle around the rue de Charonne, rue de Lappe and rue de la Roquette.

In all these areas there is a danger of petty theft. Watch your purse or wallet and be polite if you do not want trouble.

Tickets

You can get tickets for most clubs, concerts and shows at the door or box office although, as in all major cities, popular places and well-known artists get booked up very quickly so it is as well to try and buy them in advance. The FNAC bookshops sell tickets for concerts, pop and classical. Branches in the Forum des Halles (2nd level) and on the Left Bank at 136 rue de Rennes, 6e.

Other ticket agencies are listed in the Directory (pages 123). They all charge a fee.

What's Going On

To find out what's going on get the weekly *l'Officiel des Spectacles* (Wednesdays, in French); *Pariscope;* the free *Paris Selection* monthly magazine published by the Tourist Board; or the English language *Passion* magazine (published every two months by London's *Time Out* and similar in style but with more articles and fewer listings).

Where to Go

Cabaret

Can-can girls, performing seals, erupting volcanoes, bare bosoms and champagne are what the Paris cabarets are all about. They are pretty tame and although the shows pander to the male contingent of the audience, most men take their wives or at least their girlfriends. You will not see many Francophiles in the audience and the dancing girls will probably not be from Paris at all — their legs are not long enough — but it is all good fun and most of the shows are pretty spectacular.

Before the show there is often a

dinner dance which adds another couple of hundred francs to the bill. You can buy a ticket just for the 'spectacle', or 'la revue' as they call it, which usually includes at least one drink. Most cabarets have two or three shows a night, some starting after midnight. Tickets at the door are much less than the 'all-in' evening excursions sold by tour operators, even if they do include half a bottle of champagne and a bus back to your hotel. You can also buy them through agencies.

There are over 40 cabaret clubs in Paris, the following among the better known:

Crazy Horse Saloon 12 avenue George V, 8e (tel: 47.23.32.32) Theatrical extravaganza in which the evening is devoted to the admiration of the female form starring, among others, Betty Buttocks.

Folies Bergère 32 rue Richer, 9e (tel: 42.46.77.11) The Folies kicked off in the 1860s and have not changed much since, attracting a local audience (since it is a bit cheaper than the other shows) as well as busloads of visitors. Plenty of singing and dancing and frilly costumes. *Gay Paris* as it used to be without the lasers.

Lido 116 bis avenue des Champs-Elysées, 8e (tel: 45.63.11.61) On the Champs-Elysées. Expensive but worth the money for a show that costs several million dollars to put on. The spectacular effects and light show, include anything from performing elephants to erupting volcanoes and skaters. The 60 Bluebell girls are choreographed by a computer. Do not expect to be able to get a taxi when you get out unless you have reserved one in advance.

Moulin Rouge 83 boulevard de Clichy, place Blanche, 18e (tel: 46.06.00.19) Immortalised by Toulouse Lautrec, one of Paris's oldest cabarets, celebrated 100 years of the can-can in 1989, slap in the middle of the red light district.

Cinema

English language films with French sub-titles are shown at cinemas along the Champs-Elysées. Original language films are also shown at cinemas in the Latin Quarter (often oldies) and at the **Cinémathèque Française** at the Palais de Tokyo. If you want to be sure about the original language look for the initials VO. Films that have been dubbed into French will say VF. Paris is packed with cinemas. Several have more than one screen under the same roof — there are six in the **Gaumont Les Halles**, rue de Forum, Porte Rombuteau. The **Rex** (1 boulevard Poissonnière, 2e) has seven. In **La Pagode** (57 bis rue de Babylone, 7e) is a stunning Far Eastern pavilion decorated with dragons. If the film does not interest you, you can always drop in for a cup of tea. Although the commentary is in French and there are no sub-titles, if you want a

PARIS BY NIGHT

cinerama-like experience it is worth going to **La Géode** at La Villette (19e), the new 180-degree screen in a mirrored dome, with six-track stereo that wraps itself around your lateral vision. Worth the experience especially if you have children with you (open 10:00 A.M. to 9:00 P.M., closed Mondays). Do not forget to tip the usherettes. Monday nights are cheaper. Children, students and senior citizens get a reduction on all other days except Fridays and weekends.

Classical Concerts

Free (*libre*) concerts are held in churches (*église*) all over Paris. Look in one of the weekly magazines for what's on while you are there.

The National Orchestra of France also gives free concerts at: Maison de Radio France, 116 avenue du Président-Kennedy, 16e. (tel: 42.30.15.16)

Other concert venues include: Auditorium des Halles, Forum Saint-Eustache (tel: 48.04.98.01) Epicerie-Beaubourg, 12 rue du Renard, 4e (tel: 42.72.23.41)

Salle Cortot, 78 rue Cardinet, 17e (tel: 47.63.80.16) Salle Gaveau, 45 rue de la Boétie, 8e (tel: 49.53.05.07) Salle Pleyel, 252 Faubourg St-Honoré, 8e (tel: 45.61.06.30) Théâtre des Champs-Elysées, 15 avenue Montaigne, 8e (tel: 47.20.36.37) Théâtre Musical de Paris, 1 place du Châtelet, 1er (tel: 42.21.00.86)

Dance

The Opéra de Paris-Garnier at 8 rue Scribe, Place de l'Opéra, 9e (tel: 47.42.53.71) is the home of the French classical ballet in Paris. The baroque theatre holds 2,000 people who sit in splendour under the magnificent ceiling by Chagall. Even if you cannot afford a ticket you can still go in. Contemporary dance companies perform mostly in the 11e around the Bastille including: Théâtre de la Bastille (also fringe drama), 76 rue de la

Paris by night — many of the monuments and some of the bridges over the Seine are floodlit

Roquette, 11e (tel: 43.57.42.14)
Ménagerie de Verre, 12 rue
Lechevin (tel: 43.38.33.44)
The Café de la Danse, 5
passage Louis-Philippe (tel:
43.57.05.35)
Studio La Forge, 18 rue de la
Forge Royale (tel: 43.71.71.89)
Touring companies perform and
occasional dance programmes
are held at:
The American Centre, 261
boulevard Raspail, 14e (tel:
43.21.42.20)
The Casino de Paris, 16 rue de
Clichy, 9e (tel: 48.74.15.80)
Théâtre de Paris, 15 rue
Blanche, 9e (tel: 48.78.52.22)
The vast Palais de Sports, Porte
de Versailles, 15e (tel:
48.28.40.90)

Jazz

There are numerous bars in
Paris offering live jazz, from the
sleazy, smoky basements in the
Latin Quarter and around Les
Halles to big American bands
who perform in the unlikely
setting of the Méridien hotel in
the 17e and in the
huge warehouse Le Dunois out
in the 13e.
Jazz is undergoing something of
a revival in Paris. You will find
many of the clubs in
St-Germain-des-Prés on the Left
Bank, and along the partly
pedestrian-only rue des
Lombards, (1er, 4e) near
Châtelet on the Right.
Most jazz clubs do not get going
until midnight or so and stay
open until three or four in the
morning. Many also serve food.
Turn up fairly early if you want a
seat, otherwise be prepared to
stand. You usually have to pay
an amount at the door,
depending on the calibre of the
musicians, and for drinks on top
of that, though some charge an
amount for the first drink that
takes care of the entrance fee.
There are too many jazz venues
to cover them all but among the
most popular are:
Sunset (one of many in the rue
des Lombards), attracts top
musicians, small, lively and
decorated like a Métro station,
open every night from 10:30 P.M.
60 rue des Lombards, 1er.
Le Baiser Salé at number 58
offers contemporary jazz bands
as well as live soul and African
music upstairs. From 10:30 P.M.
Or try the **Duc des Lombards** at
no. 42, a small, sophisticated bar
with jazz piano on Friday and
Saturday nights as well as noisy
Afro-American Parisian
residents.
Le Petit Opportun (15 rue des
Lavandières-Sainte-Opportune,
1er), in a basement, stays open
until 3:00 A.M. if you have the
energy. If you cannot get a seat
they play tapes in the bar
upstairs. In the 10e, near
St-Lazare, real jazz enthusiasts
head for the large **New Morning
Club** (7–9 rue des Petites-
Ecuries 10e, near Brasserie Flo).
It is a bit impersonal compared
to some of the dingy basements,
and holds 400 people, but it
attracts big names in jazz, as
well as pop, salsa, African and
Brazilian bands. Concerts
usually start at 9:30 P.M.
On the Left Bank, the intimate
Bilboquet (13 rue St-Benoît)
offers jazz bands of various
nationalities who perform in a
long, narrow art-nouveau
railway carriage of a room, on
the ground floor of the hotel,

from 10:30 P.M. Near by, **Le Village** (7 rue Gozlin) on the other side of the boulevard St-Germain is where to spot new talent, and they also serve food. In the neighbouring 5e, the **Caveau de la Huchette** (5 rue de la Huchette) is one of the last true *caves*, a smoky, small, stone vaulted basement, with a dance floor, open from 9:30 P.M. to 2:30 A.M. (3:00 A.M. on Fridays) and until 4:00 A.M. on Saturdays. Over in Montparnasse in the 14e, **Le Petit Journal Montparnasse** (13 rue du Commandant-René-Mouchotte) has nightly changing bands, mostly French and well-known names. You can eat and it is open from 9:00 P.M. to 2:00 A.M. Popular, but a bit far out in the 13e, is **Le Dunois** (28 rue Dunois near the Métro Chevaleret), a vast warehouse where improvised jazz comes into its own with visiting big bands. And, in the 17e, the **Lionel Hampton Bar** of the Méridien Hotel (81 boulevard Gouvion-Saint-Cyr) offers good jazz (Monday to Saturday, 10:00 P.M. to 2:00 A.M.) in an up-market setting (also Sunday lunchtime).

Live Music

Also see Jazz (above) and Nightclubs/Discos (below). Bands play at a number of venues, some of which are huge concert halls, others are clubs where you can drink and dance. You can hear rock, salsa, African, Caribbean and plenty of other nationalities.

Rock Band Venues

Rock bands play to relatively small audiences at the **Forum des Halles**; Olympia (28 boulevard des Capucines, 9e) in the old music hall and at **Rock'n'Roll Circus**, (6 rue Caumartin, 9e).
The large venues include:
The **Palais des Congrès**, Porte Maillot, 17e where famous international bands perform in an auditorium that seats 3,700; the modern **Palais Omnisports** (8 boulevard de Bercy, 12e) which can seat 17,000 and the **Palais des Sports** at the Porte de Versailles, 15e, another enormous venue. **Le Zénith**, in the Parc de La Villette (211 boulevard Jean-Jaurès, 19e) is an inflatable stadium with seating for 6,500.

Nightclubs/Discos

Nightclubs with live bands and discos go in and out of fashion. Entry is often at the discretion of the person on the door. In some it pays off to look scruffy, at others you will not be allowed in unless you are done up to the nines or wearing suitably trendy garb. Nothing much happens this side of midnight. Your concierge (if you are staying somewhere that has one) will help choose a club and may gain you admittance for a small fee.
Clubs that seem to be fairly consistently popular or at least worth going to for the decor and atmosphere include:
Les Bains in a former Turkish bath house (7 rue du Bourg-L'Abbé, 3e). Expensive. Sometimes live rock, otherwise people-watching is fun enough. Clubby atmosphere. Upstairs restaurant.
The Rose Bon Bon (34 rue de la

Roquette, 11e), near the Bastille or **Le Gibus** (18 rue du Faubourg-du-Temple, 11e). Both with live rock bands.

Le Balajo is in an old fashioned 40s-style music hall (9 rue de la Lappe, 11e). Open Thursday, Friday, Saturday and Monday from 10:00 P.M. to 4:30 A.M. Revolving glittery globe above the dance-floor, with a band on a sequinned balcony. Saturday afternoon for old-time dancing. Evenings for up-to-the-minute stuff. **Le Tango** (13 rue au Maire, 3e) is another venue for real dancing whether it is reggae or a rhumba. Open Wednesday to Saturday.

Le Palace (8 rue du Faubourg-Montmartre, 9e) attracts a mixed crowd of all ages, a big popular disco still going strong after ten years or so. Various theme nights. If you eat first in the downstairs restaurant you get free entrance. Dress up. Open nightly.

La Locomotive (90 boulevard de Clichy, 18e) is on three floors, much of it under the Moulin Rouge. Different levels and dance floors. Trendy crowd.

Club Olivia Valere (40 rue du Colisée, 8e) is open until dawn for older sophisticated Parisians who have moved on from **Régine's** (49 rue de Ponthieu, 8e) piano bar, dance floor and restaurant. Expensive and can be difficult to get in.

L'Atmosphère (45 rue François 1er, 8e), is just as sophisticated, but you may be lucky and be allowed in.

Opera

The Paris Opéra season is from

The Lido on the Champs Elysées has the most extravagant floor show

the end of September to mid-July. For tickets apply to: L'Opéra de Paris Bastille, 2 bis, place de la Bastille, 12e (tel: 40.01.16.16). This is the new home of the Opéra de Paris. The Palais Garnier (the former State Opera House) in the Place de l'Opéra (near Galeries Lafayette) is now solely the home of the French Ballet (see **Dance**).

Opera is also performed at the Epicerie Beaubourg (see Classical Concerts) and at the Opéra-Comique at the Salle Favard, 5 rue Favart, 2e. Tel: 42.96.12.20. Other venues include the Théâtre du Châtelet, 1 place du Châtelet, 1er (tel: 40.28.28.40) and Théâtre du Lierre, 22 rue du Chevaleret, 13e (tel: 45.86.55.83).

PARIS BY NIGHT

Pigalle — the seedy side of Paris

Prostitutes

Prostitution is not illegal but soliciting is. The main areas are around Pigalle (9e and 18e), the rue St-Denis near the Forum des Halles, around the Opéra, behind the Madeleine in rue de Sèze, in the rue Daunou in the 2e, the rue de la Gaîté near Montparnasse in the 14e and in the avenue Foch in the 16e.

Sex Shows — The Pigalle

Paris has its share of sleazy strip clubs, tattoo parlours, and live, or 'life' as they call them, sex shows. Many of them are private. Pigalle is where most of them are, in and around the boulevard Clichy, in the 9e *arrondissement* and just over the border into the 18e, which, with its narrow streets and dead-end alleyways, is even less salubrious. It is not all nightclubs — there are plenty of boutiques (with names like Derrière les Fagots) and hotels. In case you are offered a hotel in this area, the streets to avoid are those leading north off the boulevard Clichy, the rue Frochot, rue Henri-Monnier, rue Lafferière, rue Notre-Dame de Lorette, rue Chaptal and rue Blanche. It is not unheard of for tour operators 'innocently' to offer hotels in Pigalle, eulogising their proximity to the Moulin Rouge and Montmartre and for visitors to be shocked and angry to discover their proximity to the seedier side of Paris. Be warned and check out the address before you accept the booking.

Business in Pigalle apparently is not booming. The locals blame it on AIDS frightening off the tourists and the TGV high speed train which denies errant businessmen the old excuse to spend a night in the city and whisks them home to the suburbs in time for cocoa.

Other areas: Less sordid, with a handful of sex shows and plenty of neons, is the rue St-Denis near the Forum des Halles, some of the streets around the Bastille (11e) and the rue de la Gaîté near Montparnasse (14e). The sex shows are still offered but alongside other possibilities from art galleries to discos and jazz clubs.

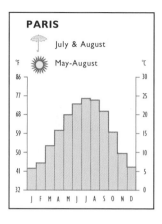

Left: painters in Montmartre

THE WEATHER

See chart.

WHEN TO GO

Major trade fairs, fashion shows and art exhibitions govern how full or empty Paris is at any one time. The Office de Tourisme advise avoiding: mid January, early February, first half of March, end of April, second half of May, June, September, October and mid November when it can be difficult to find a hotel room (also see Accommodation, page 79). Other than that, the quietest time is generally March to May and November. Autumn can be pretty wet and New Year chilly and windy.

If you're planning to shop, a good time to visit is after Christmas for the January sales. If the purpose of your visit is to sample the restaurants don't forget to book well ahead and avoid July and August when many of the best restaurants close for their annual vacations. If you're planning a short stay, include Friday rather than Monday when many galleries and museums are shut.

EVENTS

The French Government Tourist Office produce a free leaflet *Saison de Paris* listing major events and exhibitions.

January
Fashion collections

February
World Tourist and Travel Show
Fashion collections

March
Agricultural Show

April
Paris Fair

EVENTS

May

Paris Air Show, Le Bourget
(every two years)
Paris Festival (until end of June)

June

Annual Flower Show — Bois des
Vincennes
French Tennis Championships
Paris Villages Festival

July

Bastille Day (14th). Fireworks
and military display, marking
the anniversary of the French
Revolution
Finish of the Tour de France
(last Sunday, Champs Elysées)
Fashion collections
Festival Estival (concerts until
mid-Sept)

The Paris Marathon, usually in May

August

Parisians go on vacation

September

International Contemporary Arts
Exhibition, Grand Palais (until
end October/early November)

October

Concerts in churches. Jazz
Festival. Festival of Dance

November

Concerts in churches. Jazz
Festival
Armistice Day (11th). Military
displays at the Arc de Triomphe
Antiques Fair, Espace Austerlitz

December

International Boat Show

HOW TO BE A LOCAL

In a world where life is becoming increasingly humdrum and cosmopolitan, national traits and characteristics are under serious threat. Paris has been no less subject to this trend than anywhere else, so being a local is not the specialised art it once was; but its attractions and its population remain unique. A lot of the chic has gone, especially among the younger generation, though older Parisians are still often fairly unmistakable, either through their easy elegance or through essential accoutrements like berets.

Parisians rich and poor have always liked their food and know exactly what they want. See them at their best in the street markets, where they banter and haggle.

Popular pastimes include short strolls through the parks, by the river and along the boulevards, the last being punctuated by stops at sidewalk bars and cafés. These have traditionally been favourite spots to see and be seen, particularly those on the Champs Elysées and the boulevard St-Germain. But these places are usually quite expensive, and the older locals will tell you that there's much less to see, fewer fashions to turn heads, less chic to admire, less 'proper' Paris. But style there still is, and correct service from smartly attired staff is something that Parisians still demand and still generally get. This applies also to restaurants, where the scene is inevitably slipping into fast gear. But right-minded locals ensure the continued existence of back-street bistros, where good simple French food is still available. In the more up-scale establishments, a detailed knowledge of and close interest in the menu marks out Parisians. Sunday lunchtime often brings three generations together *en famille* and it is fascinating to see that even the very young and the very old will debate long and hard about what to order.

Parisians are effusive in their greetings and always seem to find time for a conversation. Topics are much the same as anywhere else, with the addition of an obsession with their health.

In brief, to be a local, you need to be enthusiastic and outgoing, something which should come fairly naturally as soon as Paris has begun to cast its spell.

Feeding the pigeons in the park, a pastime for young and old

CHILDREN

Paris does not cater particularly
well to young children although
older ones will enjoy the main
sites and under 18's get in free
to National Museums. There are
no reductions on the Métro or
buses although under 3's are
free. Few restaurants have
highchairs, though many will
serve small portions if you ask
them but there are so many
fast-food restaurants that finding
cheap snacks is easy. If you are
taking a baby you will have no
problems buying disposable
diapers or jars of baby food and
you can hire a babysitter if you
want a night out without them. It
does not take long for all
children to discover that Paris is
different and for school-age
children to try out their French.
Children of all ages will enjoy:
riding up the escalator outside
the Beaubourg and the free
street shows in the piazza
outside; taking the elevator (or
even the steps) up the Eiffel
Tower; climbing to the top of
Notre-Dame Cathedral or the
Arc de Triomphe and riding in
a *bateau mouche* along the
Seine. Remember that as well as
under 18's getting into National
Museums free, on Sundays
many museums are free to
everyone. There are a number
of playgrounds in the main
parks, many with puppet shows
(see below), although
unfortunately you are not
allowed to let children run on
the grass.

The French are, of course,
obsessed with dressing their
little darlings *à la mode*. There
are some superb shops for

Parisian children dress à la mode.
*Kenzo's boutique for children is in
the place des Victoires*

children's clothes, including a
Baby Dior, Kenzo for kids, and
lovely boutiques in the rue
Jacob (6e). The department
stores, especially Monoprix and
Prisunic are cheaper, though
not that cheap, as in France
there is tax on children's clothes
of 18.6 percent.

Babies

You can rent a stroller (or a crib
or hire a babysitter) from Allo
Maman Poule. Tel: 47.47.78.78
(24 hrs). For babysitting only try
Kid Service (closed Sunday).
Tel: 42.96.04.16. or ABABA La
Maman en Plus Tel: 43.22.22.11.
You can buy familiar brands of
baby food and formula and
disposable diapers (*couches à
jeter*) in supermarkets and
pharmacies.

Places to Visit

Most of the places listed below

have also been covered in different sections so cross reference under *Directory* (pages 103-123), Museums, Parks and Gardens, and Excursions from Paris in *What to See* (pages 21-44). Check in *Pariscope* or *l'Officiel des Spectacles* for the opening hours and times of special shows.

AQUABOULEVARD, 15e
A large park with an artificial lake where you can swim and sail boats, near the Porte de Sévres.

... there's plenty in the streets and squares of Paris to tempt the young photographer

BEAUBOURG/Georges Pompidou Centre, 4e
Rues Rambuteau, Saint-Martin and Beaubourg
Make a beeline for the Beaubourg even if you do not want to take the children into one of the changing exhibitions or the National Museum of Modern Art. On Wednesdays and Saturdays they run children's workshops with English-speaking playleaders. There is also a children's library, open in the afternoons from 1:00 to 7:00 P.M. with an English section for 6–12's. The square outside is a free entertainment zone. There may

CHILDREN

be jugglers, musicians, artists, portrait painters, or clowns to keep them occupied.

The ride up the outside of the Pompidou Centre, on the glassed-in escalator, is free and fun with good views.
Métro: Hôtel-de-Ville, Rambuteau. *RER* Châtelet-les-Halles.
Closed: Tuesdays.

CITÉ DES SCIENCES ET DE L'INDUSTRIE, La Villette, 19e
30 avenue Corentin Cariou
Vast hands-on museum on the site of the city slaughterhouse, with computers, robots, machinery to work and buttons to press in an area several times the size of the Beaubourg. Unfortunately few of the instructions are in English except on a few computers, but headsets with a commentary are available in English. On the premis that most children do not read instructions anyway, there is enough for them to work out for themselves to make it worth a visit. There is a dragon slide in the park behind the Cité and a huge mirrored dome, La Géode, shows 180-degree projection films (in French). One fee to get into the Museum but extra charges for the Inventorium and the Planetarium.
Métro: Porte de la Villette (20 minutes from central Paris) or trips by barge up the canals (see page 25-26).
Open: Tuesday, Thursday and Friday: 10:00 A.M. to 6:00 P.M. Wednesday, noon to 9:00 P.M., Saturday, Sunday and holidays: noon to 8:00 P.M.
Closed: Monday

Children as well as adults will enjoy the Musée d'Orsay's Impressionist paintings

EIFFEL TOWER, 7e
Champs de Mars
You can get an elevator up to the first, second and third stages. On the first floor there is an audio-visual of the history of the tower which was built in 1889 for the World Exhibition.
Métro: Trocadéro, Bir-Hakeim
Open: 10:00 A.M. to 11:00 P.M. (midnight Friday, Saturday and holidays, April to early September and daily in July and August)

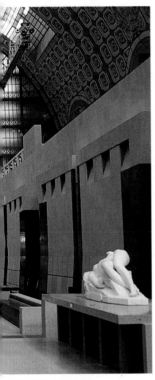

help with identification. 686 feet (209m) high. Open-air terrace on the 59th floor.
Métro: Montparnasse-Bienvenüe
Open: 10:00 A.M. to 10:00 P.M. (11:00 P.M. Friday, Saturday and holidays; daily from April to September)

MUSÉE D'ORSAY, 7e
1 rue de Bellechase
Magnificent art collection in the former railway station. Works by the Impressionist painters Renoir, Monet and Degas on the top floor. A good introduction to some of the world's most famous paintings. Pleasant views across the Seine to the Right Bank from the terrace by the café on the top floor. Stunningly palatial restaurant on the first floor.
Métro: Solférino
Open: 10:00 A.M. to 5:30 P.M. (till 9:15 P.M. Thursday); Sunday 9:00 A.M. to 6:00 P.M.
Closed: Monday

MUSÉE DES ARTS AFRICAINS ET OCÉANIENS, 12e
293 avenue Daumesnil
At the entrance of the Bois de Vincennes. It has a tropical aquarium as well as displays of the arts and crafts of Africa and Oceania and you could combine it with the zoo.
Métro: Porte Dorée
Open: 10:00 A.M. to noon and 1:30 P.M. to 5:30 P.M. (weekends 10:00 A.M. to 6:00 P.M.)
Closed: Tuesdays

LE PARC ASTERIX
A new leisure park with 100 attractions and six 'worlds' to explore; among these are the world of Asterix, Ancient Rome and the world of the imagination. Reached by shuttle service from Charles-de-Gaulle RER station. 24 miles (38km) from Paris, near Roissy Airport.
Open: May-October daily. Wednesdays and weekends in Winter.

MONTPARNASSE TOWER, 15e
Elevator up to the 56th floor in 38 seconds, for great views of the capital with telescopes to

PARC OCEANIQUE COUSTEAU, 1er
Forum des Halles
A great adventure for children. Journeying through space, plunging to Earth, into the sea, you explore the creatures of the

CHILDREN

The pond in the Tuileries Gardens is the place for sailing boats

deep from the safety of your vessel. Back on the surface, climb inside a life-size model of a blue whale, or learn about a variety of marine life from hands-on video displays.
Métro: Les Halles
RER: Chatelet-Les-Halles
Open: daily (except Monday) noon to 7:00 P.M.

Boats
A boat ride along the Seine in a *bateau mouche* or *vedette* is well worth doing, just for the fun of it and also because most of the well-known monuments can

be seen along the banks. Boats are large, covered and there are English commentaries. They are run by different companies and leave from various points including: Pont de l'Alma, Pont d'Iéna (opposite the Eiffel Tower), and Pont Neuf (near the Louvre). Night-time excursions to see the illuminations are more expensive, as are boats with tea or dinner on board. (See also **Directory** section).
For barge rides along the

canals to La Villette, see pages 25 and 26.

Parks and Playgrounds

The Jardin d'Acclimatation in the Bois de Boulogne, 16e is the best place to take young children but it is not cheap. Take the Métro to Sablons or to Porte Maillot (afternoons only). If your children want a ride on a little train, choose an afternoon on a Wednesday, weekend or school vacation. Plenty to do and go on (rides, bowling, miniature golf, miniature farm and paddle boats down the enchanted river). All the rides are priced individually. The Bois de Boulogne has miniature golf, boating and bowling and you can rent bikes to ride through the woods.

There are **children's playgrounds** in the Parc Monceau, 17e (*Métro:* Monceau), and the Parc Floral (route de la Pyramide near the Bois de Vincennes) has a children's theatre (Astral) as well as plenty of things for children to do especially on summer weekends. (*Métro:* Château de Vincennes) The Jardin des Plantes, 5e (*Métro:* Gare d'Austerlitz) has a mini zoo, aquarium and a maze. The Luxembourg Gardens, 6e has a playground, pony rides, toy boats and puppet theatre (*RER:* Luxembourg) and the Tuileries Gardens, 1er (*Métro:* Tuileries, Concorde) has the famous octagonal pond on which Parisian children sail their boats.

There are also puppet shows in the Buttes-Chaumont park on Wednesday and weekend afternoons at 3:15 and 4:15 P.M.

in the Champs de Mars near the Eiffel Tower (*Métro:* Ecole-Militaire) and in the gardens at the Rond-Point north of the Champs-Elysées on Wednesdays and weekends at 3:00 P.M., 4:00 P.M. and 5:00 P.M. If you are shopping in the Forum des Halles there is a children's playground, with babysitters, near St-Eustache. In the park behind the Cité des Sciences et de l'Industrie there is a popular dragon slide. Also at La Villette there is a rock concert stadium, the Zenith and a 180-degree projection cinema screen La Géode, for films (though only in French).

Skating

Roller-skating rink in the Parc Monceau, 17e and La Main Jaune at the Porte de Champerret, also in the 17e.
There is an ice-skating rink in the Buttes-Chaumont, 30 rue Edouard Pailleron, 19e.
Métro: Bolivar.

Swimming

There is an outdoor pool, Molitor, in the Bois de Boulogne in summer.
Métro: Porte-d'Auteuil. And another, the Piscine Deligny, on the Left Bank of the Seine near the Musée d'Orsay. Indoor and outdoor pools are listed in *Pariscope* under *Piscines* (swimming pools) and in the **Directory**, page 121.

Zoos

Nothing very exciting. There is a small zoo in the Jardin des Plantes, rue Cuvier, 5e and one in the Bois de Vincennes, avenue de St Maurice, 12e.
Métro: Porte Dorée

TIGHT BUDGET

Paris need not be expensive. If you are on a budget there are plenty of cheap hotels and youth hostel accommodation. When you arrive look for the *hôtesses de Paris* at the railway station or at the airport. They will tell you which hotels have vacancies and generally point you in the right direction.

• Students can get reductions with an International Student Card. You must have proof that you are a full time student, a passport sized photo and 30F (currently). Go to the Council for International Education Exchange. 49 rue Pierre-Charron, 8e. Tel: 43.59.23.69. With it you can get reductions to museums, films and on public transportation.

• Don't buy a single ticket when travelling on the Métro or on buses. It is cheaper to buy a book (*carnet*) of tickets and invest in one of the cheap cards (see Tickets, page 114). The Carte Jeune entitles under 25s to a 50 per cent reduction on the trains in France between June and September, for example.

• Use your student card to get reductions on admission charges to museums or else join the lines on Sundays when many offer free admission. Alternatively, buy a *Carte Inter-Musées*, offering unlimited visits to major museums and monuments for a single payment. Available from museums, métro stations and tourist information offices.

• The cheapest restaurants are *Les Selfs* (self-service) in large department stores. Otherwise follow the local students on the Left Bank to cheap restaurants in the 5e *arrondissement*. There are specific student restaurants in the 5e and 6e or you can buy take-out (Greek mostly) from the rue Huchette, 5e.

• Restaurants have their menus displayed outside — those with fixed prices for two or three courses are the best value. Drink house wine out of a jug or carafe.

Le Trumilou has been offering cheap meals for some 100 years

• Avoid expensive bars in popular streets like the boulevard St-Germain and around Beaubourg. If you are thirsty head for a back street bar. Beer drinkers should ask for *une demi* (half) or *pression* (draft) and it is worth remembering that fizzy mineral water can be more expensive than wine!

• The cheapest places to buy clothes are Monoprix and Prisunic department stores, but the best 'designer' selection is at Galeries Lafayette. There are also discount 'designer' shops where they sell off samples and last year's fashion.

DIRECTORY

Airports

Orly Airport
Information: Tel: (1) 49.75.15.15
Twelve and a half miles (20km)
to the south of Paris.
Travel into Paris
The Orly/Rail (*RER:* line C) will
take you to Gare d'Austerlitz
and stations on the Left Bank.
Trains leave every 15 minutes
from 5:30 A.M. to 11:00 P.M. and
take about 35 minutes.
There are two bus possibilities.
The cheaper Express Bus goes
direct to Denfert-Rochereau
Métro near Montparnasse in the
14e on the Left Bank. It takes
about half-an-hour and buses
leave every 15 minutes from
6:05 A.M. to 11:00 P.M. Or you can
get the Air France bus to the
Aerogare des Invalides in the
7e, which is a bit nearer the
centre, or to the Gare
Montparnasse, avenue du

*The traffic speeding around the
Arc de Triomphe is terrifying. Cross
at your peril*

Maine, 17e. Buses leave every
12 minutes and the journey
should take about 35 minutes.

Roissy-Charles de Gaulle Airport
Information: Tel: (1) 48.62.22.80
Fourteen miles (23km) to the
northeast of Paris.
Travel into Paris
The free airport bus will take
you to the *RER* train station for
connections to Paris. This is the
quickest and most direct route.
In 40 minutes you will be at the
Gare du Nord from where you
can either get a taxi (sometimes
there are lines so be warned) or
change onto the Métro. You can
also continue by train to
Châtelet-les-Halles which is
nearer to the centre and from
where it is easier to get a taxi.
Trains leave at 15-minute

intervals between 5:30 A.M. and 11:00 P.M. The direct Air France bus (every 15 minutes) will drop you at Porte Maillot (lower level of the Palais des Congrès) in the 17e, or at the place de Charles-de-Gaulle-Etoile (avenue Carnot) from where you can get a taxi or the Métro. Buses run between 5:45 A.M. and 11:00 P.M. You should allow at least one hour on the bus.

Cheaper and slower are the regular buses: no. 350 to the Gare du Nord and the Gare de l'Est and the 351 to the place de la Nation. Allow at least 50 minutes by taxi.

Camping

You can camp in the Bois de Boulogne all year round: Route du Bord de l'Eau. Arrive early in summer as the site can be full by midday. An international camping ticket is necessary. Tel: 45.24.30.00.

Car Breakdown

If your car breaks down, the Paris 24-hour repair service can be contacted at: 43.06.22.31 or 47.07.99.99

Car Rental

Agencies include:
Autorent Tel: 45.54.22.45
Avis Tel: 46.09.92.12
Budget-Milleville Tel: 05.10.00.01
Europcar Tel: 30.43.82.82
Hertz Tel: 47.88.51.51
Inter Touring Service Tel: 45.88.52.37 including cars for the disabled
Snac Tel: 45.53.33.91
Thrifty Tel: 05.16.02.75
In order to rent a car you must produce a current driving licence (which you have held for at least a year) and you must also produce your passport.

If you want to get anywhere in a hurry, go by Métro. If not, sit in a café until after the rush hour.

Depending upon the company, the minimum age requirement will be 21 or 25.

Chauffeur Driven Cars

If you want a driver contact:
Executive Car Carey Limousine
Tel: 42.65.54.20
London Cab in Paris Tel:
43.70.18.18
Murdoch Associés (bi-lingual drivers who will also act as personal assistants). All cars have telephones. Tel: 47.20.00.21 or in the UK: 0342 316428
Societé des Chauffeurs Tel:
46.34.77.07

Crime

Petty crime is high in Paris. Watch your purse or wallet on the Métro, in busy tourist areas like the Beaubourg and the Champs-Elysées and in lines for museums. Be wary of seemingly innocent, scruffy-looking children — they work the streets in gangs fleecing innocent tourists. Do not leave valuables visible in your car.

Domestic Travel

Driving in Paris

Just stand at the Arc de Triomphe or in the middle of the place de la Concorde and you will be convinced that all Parisians are practising for Le Mans. Cornering on one wheel with a squeal of brakes is par for the course. You must, of course, drive on the right and the speed limit is 60 km/h (37 mph) in built up areas, 90 km/h (56 mph) in other areas, 110 km/h (68 mph) on dual-lane highways and 130 km/h (81 mph) on motorways (with 110 km/h [68 mph] limit on urban stretches). The speed limit on the

périphérique is 80 km/h (50 mph). There are also wet weather limits. A *minimum* speed limit of 80 km/h (50 mph) is in force on the outside lane of motorways during daytime visibility.
You must not exceed 90 km/h (56 mph) if you have held a full driving licence for less than a year. An international driving licence is not compulsory.
As you approach the city do not on any account drive straight in. Take the *périphérique,* the ring road, watching carefully for the nearest *porte* (exit) to your ultimate destination.

Parking If you are driving to Paris the best idea is to leave your car in one of the long-term parking lots outside the *périphérique.* There are also parking lots in the city but they are more expensive. Remember that it is prohibited to leave a vehicle for more than 24 consecutive hours in the same place in Paris.
Do not assume that because you bear foreign number plates you will be immune from the boot, the tow-away truck or the wrath of the *pervenches* (blue-uniformed traffic wardens). If you are unfortunate enough to be booted or your car is removed to the *fourrière* (police pound), ask the nearest *policier* or Commissariat de Police how to get it out. In the centre there are parking meters, or machines dispensing tickets on street corners. Street parking prohibitions are indicated by yellow markings on the curb, or by street signs. Unfamiliar road signs may include those stating

that parking is allowed on only one side of a street or that the gutters are due for a night cleaning. As for parking itself, nowhere in the world makes better use of the bumper. Parisians squeeze themselves into the tiniest parking places, simply by shoving the car in front and behind out of the way. Should you be unfortunate enough to be one of them, you will find it impossible to get out of your well-earned space. Paris is a relatively small city and the Métro is quick and convenient to use. Traffic is often very heavy indeed. A car is not really necessary.

Gasoline In France gas is graded as *Normale* or *Super* and visiting motorists should be careful to use a grade in the recommended range as the performance of many modern engines depends on the correct grade of gasoline being used. Additionally, aś unleaded gas is also being sold, it is important to purchase the correct gas. If a car designed to run on leaded gasoline is filled with unleaded gasoline it will do no immediate harm, provided it is the correct octane rating and the next fill is of leaded gas.

Gasoline (leaded) Essence Normale (90 octane) and Essence Super (98 octane) grades.

Gasoline (unleaded) is sold in France as Essence Super (95 octane). Pumps dispensing unleaded gasoline are clearly marked with a sticker *super sans plomb* (super grade unleaded).

In France, as in all European countries, gasoline is supplied and priced in litres. The minimum amount that will be supplied is usually five litres (one U.S. gallon = approx 3.8 litres). You will find all the familiar brand-names in Paris, and will have no difficulty in obtaining fuel, but if you travel to rural locations you should keep a full tank.If a full tank is required ask the pump attendant to *Faites-le-plein, s'il vous plaît.*

Road Signs Most road signs are internationally agreed and the majority will be familiar to motorists.

Watch for road markings — do not cross a solid white or yellow line marked on the road centre.

Rules of the Road In France, drive on the right and pass on the left, as in the U.S. In addition, you must give way to traffic approaching from the right *(priorité à droite)* in built-up areas. Outside built-up areas, all main roads have right of way *(passage protégé).*

Seat Belts If your car is fitted with seat belts it is compulsory to wear them. Failure to do so could result in an *on-the-spot* fine.

Boats

They may be clichéd but the glass-topped *bateaux-mouches* (also called *vedettes*) that chug up and down the Seine are one of the best ways of seeing Paris. Many of her most famous monuments are visible along the bank: the Eiffel Tower, the Louvre, Notre-Dame Cathedral, the Île de la Cité, and the new

Lunch on board a bâteau mouche. Be warned − it will be expensive

Musée d'Orsay among them. The cheapest way to do it is the straightforward tour (there is a commentary in English). Some boats also serve tea, or you can pay around ten times as much to have lunch on board, or even more for dinner and a light show.

There are a number of different companies leaving from different points along the Seine. Take the Métro to any one of: Pont Neuf, Alma Marceau, or Bir-Hakeim/Iéna. Boats leave regularly. The Tourist Office (Champs-Elysées, main stations and the Eiffel Tower − in summer) have brochures and timetables.

Buses

Buses are one way of seeing the city (especially route 24),

although traffic can be very heavy. Bus stops show the numbers of the buses that stop there. There is a map of the stops *en route*, and you can get maps of the whole system from Métro stations, bus terminals and the Tourist Office. You may also see a ticket machine. Some stops have a ticket machine for lining up, since the French seem to be incapable of standing in a straight line. Take one as soon as you arrive at the stop. Also, do not forget to ring the bell when you want to get off as the bus will not stop automatically. Buses start at 6:30 A.M. Some routes end at around 9:00 P.M., others run until 12:30 A.M. There are special night buses (*noctambus*) (you hail them) which run in various directions every hour between 1:30 A.M. and 5:30 A.M. from the place du Châtelet. A special *Montmartrobus* tours the Montmartre district.

You can also get excursions on the buses to places like Versailles which work out much cheaper than taking one of the sightseeing bus tours. Bus tickets are the same as those for the Métro although they are divided into fare stages. You need one ticket for a journey of one or two fare stages and two or more tickets for three or more fare stages.

Bus Tours

Several companies offer sightseeing bus tours of the city. Some are double-decker buses with huge glass windows. Commentaries are either through headphones which you set to the language you want or through multi-lingual guides. There are several possibilities, depending on how much time you have to spare, including tours of museums, and visits to nightspots like the Lido which may include a meal. The organised tours are a lot more expensive than making your own arrangements.

You can also buy bus excursions to sites outside Paris including Versailles, Malmaison Giverny and Chartres. You can make your own way there much cheaper by public transportation (see Excursions from Paris, pages 41-44). For your money you get a guide, and a commentary or piped music on board the bus, although often only a limited amount of time in the place. You should book in advance, either by telephone or by calling into the office in person:

Cityrama, 4 place des Pyramides, 1er. Tel: 42.60.30.14
Paris Vision, 214 rue de Rivoli, 1er and 1 rue Auber, 9e. Tel: 42.60.31.25 and 42.60.30.01
For national coach tours. Tel: VIA International 42.05.12.10

Canals

You can take a barge along the canals running through and out of Paris. La Villette and the Cité des Sciences et de l'Industrie is one of the most popular destinations. Tickets and information from:
Canauxrama, (canal St Martin). Tel: 46.07.13.13
Quiztour (Paris Canal), (Seine and canal St Martin). Tel: 42.40.96.97

Métro

The entrances to many of Paris's Métro stations can be spotted in the streets by their distinctive art nouveau designs and huge M signs. The various lines are called by the names of the stations at each end, the *correspondances* are the points at which lines join. Look for signs for the relevant *direction* you are travelling in and follow the colour-coded and numbered lines. Changing lines is quite easy once you get the hang of it. There are usually large plans of the whole network outside each station, some with illuminated buttons which are fun to operate. A map of the Métro will be found on page 110, and there is also a Métro map on the back of the free map of Paris from the Tourist Office. Outside some stations (numbers increasing daily) there are computerised route finders called SITU (*système d'information de trajets urbains*). You tap in the name of the street you want to get to and get a print-out of the quickest way to get there, including walking. Most stations are quite cheerful inside with gaily coloured plastic seats and matching tiles, plus videos to watch to while away the time. The Louvre station is an extension of the Museum, with works of art displayed in cabinets along the platform. There are the usual street musicians but in Paris they do it in style, playing jazz and classical music on trains as well as off. Some of them may well be students from the Conservatoire National. It is forbidden to smoke. There is a warning siren just before the doors close and you release the door yourself to

A bus ride can take in the major sites and be much cheaper than an official tour

get off.
There are two classes of ticket, first and second. Before 9:00 A.M. and after 5:00 P.M. passengers holding a second-class ticket are allowed to travel in first-class carriages. First is generally less crowded.
The first Métro is at 5:30 A.M. The last at 12:30 A.M. As in most other cities, it is inadvisable to get into an empty carriage alone, especially late at night.

RER
The RER is the fast suburban service which will take you to places like Versailles (much cheaper than an organised excursion). The lines are divided into sections and the cost of a ticket (you can use the same ones as on the buses or the Métro within the metropolitan area) varies according to the number of sections you cross. The RER goes to Charles-de-Gaulle and Orly airports.
(Also see pages 110 and 112).

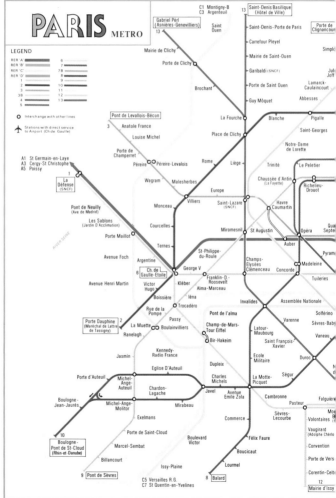

© TCS

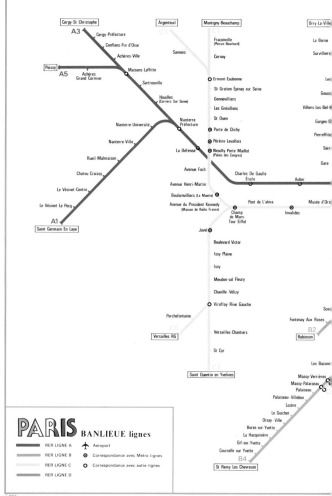

Cergy-St Christophe
A3
Cergy-Préfecture
Conflans-Fin d'Oise
Achères-Ville
Poissy
A5
Achères
Grand Cormier
Maisons-Laffitte
Sartrouville
Houilles
(Carriers Sur Seine)
Nanterre-Université
Nanterre
Préfecture
Nanterre-Ville
La Défense
Rueil-Malmaison
Avenue Foch
Chatou-Croissy
Le Vésinet-Centre
Avenue Henri-Martin
Boulainvilliers (La Muette)
Le Vésinet-Le Pecq
Avenue du President Kennedy
(Maison de Radio France)
A1
Saint Germain En Laye
Javel
Boulevard Victor
Issy Plaine
Issy
Meudon-val Fleury
Chaville-Vélizy
Viroflay Rive Gauche
Porchefontaine
Versailles RG
Versailles-Chantiers
St Cyr
Saint Quentin en Yvelines

Argenteuil

Montigny-Beauchamp
Fraconville
(Plessis Bouchard)
Cernay
Sannois
Ermont-Eaubonne
St Gratien Epinay sur Seine
Gennevilliers
Les Grésillons
St Ouen
Porte de Clichy
Pereire-Levallois
Neuilly-Porte Maillot
(Palais des Congres)
Charles De Gaulle
Étoile
Pont de L'alma
Champ
de Mars-
Tour Eiffel
Invalides

Orry-La-Ville
La Borne
Survilliers
Les
Gouss
Villiers-Les-Bel-
Garges-St
Pierrefitte
Sain
Gare
Auber
Musée d'Ors

Sceau
Fontenay Aux Roses
B2
Robinson

Les Bacon
Massy-Verrières
Massy-Palaiseau
Palaiseau
Palaiseau-Villebon
Lozère
Le Guichet
Orsay-Ville
Bures-sur-Yvette
La Hacquinière
Gif-sur-Yvette
Courcelle sur Yvette
B4
St Remy Les Chevreuse

PARIS BANLIEUE lignes

— RER LIGNE A   ✈ Aeroport
— RER LIGNE B   ⊚ Correspondance avec Metro lignes
— RER LIGNE C   ⊙ Correspondance avec autre lignes
— RER LIGNE D

© TCS

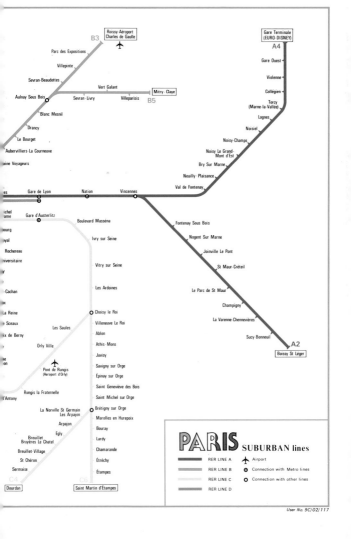

B3

Roissy-Aéroport
Charles de Gaulle

Parc des Expositions

Villepinte

Sevran-Beaudottes

Vert Galant

Mitry - Claye

Aulnay Sous Bois

Sevran - Livry

Villeparisis

B5

Blanc Mesnil

Drancy

Le Bourget

Aubervilliers-La Courneuve

aine Voyageurs

es

Gare de Lyon

Nation

Vincennes

ichel
ame

Gare d'Austerlitz

Boulevard Masséna

bourg

Ivry sur Seine

yal

Rochereau

niversitaire

y

-Cachan

xx

La Reine

Vitry sur Seine

Les Ardoines

e Sceaux

Les Saules

ix de Berny

Orly Ville

ie
on

Pont de Rungis
(Aeroport d'Orly)

Rungis la Fraternelle

d'Antony

La Norville St Germain
Les Arpajon

Arpajon

Egly

Breuillet
Bruyères Le Chatel

Breuillet-Village

St Chéron

Sermaise

C4

Dourdan

Choisy le Roi

Villeneuve Le Roi

Ablon

Athis-Mons

Juvisy

Savigny sur Orge

Épinay sur Orge

Saint Geneviève des Bois

Saint Michel sur Orge

Brétigny sur Orge

Marolles en Hurepoix

Bouray

Lardy

Chamarande

Étréchy

Étampes

C6

Saint Martin d'Étampes

Gare Terminale
(EURO-DISNEY)

A4

Gare Ouest

Violenne

Collégien

Torcy
(Marne-la-Vallée)

Lognes

Noisiel

Noisy-Champs

Noisy Le Grand-
Mont d'Est

Bry Sur Marne

Neuilly-Plaisance

Val de Fontenay

Fontenay Sous Bois

Nogent Sur Marne

Joinville Le Pont

St Maur-Créteil

Le Parc de St Maur

Champigny

La Varenne-Chennevières

Sucy-Bonneuil

A2

Boissy St Léger

PARIS SUBURBAN lines

RER LINE A	✈ Airport
RER LINE B	⊙ Connection with Metro lines
RER LINE C	○ Connection with other lines
RER LINE D	

The main lines are:
Ligne A:
Saint-Germain-en-Laye to
Boissy-Saint-Léger or Torcy
Marne La Vallée
Ligne B: Saint-Rémy-les-
Chevreuse to Gare du Nord/
Roissy (airport) or Mitry-Claye
Ligne Massy-Palaiseau, Vers
Dourdan or Vers St-Martin-
d'Étampes to Versailles or St-
Quentin-en-Yvelines.

Taxis

Taxis can be hailed if you are
lucky enough to see one with
both lights on the roof showing.
One lit means it is occupied.
You must not hail a taxi within 20
yards (18 m) of a stand or *tête
de station*. All taxis have meters
and there are surcharges for
luggage, late nights and
Sundays. Pick-up charges from
and to stations are higher than
from the nearest street corner.
There are also surcharges after
10:00 P.M. and before 6:30 A.M.,
for heavy luggage and on
Sundays. Lines can be long,
especially at the Gare du Nord.
You are expected to tip around
10–15 per cent. It is sometimes
very difficult indeed to get a taxi.
Your hotel or restaurant will
usually call for one but even at
top hotels like the de Crillon you
have to wait outside in a line like
everyone else. Taxis will seldom
take more than three people. You
can try to book a cab in advance
by telephoning:
G7 Radio: 47.39.47.39
Alpha Taxi: 47.30.23.23
Taxi Bleus: 42.02.42.02
Taxi Radio Etoile: 42.70.41.41
If you have a complaint, address
it to:
Service des Taxis de la

*The Paris Métro is fast, clean
and efficient. The colour-coded
and numbered lines are simple to
follow*

Préfecture de Police, 36 rue des
Morillons, 75015 Paris.

Tickets (Subway or Bus)

If you are staying only a short
while, the cheapest way to
travel is to buy a *carnet* or book
of ten tickets rather than to buy
a ticket for each individual
journey. You only need one
ticket for each RER or Métro
journey regardless of how long
it is or how many times you
change trains. The same tickets
can be used on the buses (see
above). You should buy them
from the booking office or from
tabacs, slot machines or bus
terminals. A *Paris-Visite* ticket
for 3 or 5 days is worth it only if
you plan a lot of travelling. It
gives you unlimited travel on

the Métro, RER, SNCF suburban services and buses. There are two types of ticket: Paris and nearby suburbs, and Paris and the Ile de France (including Versailles and Orly and Roissy airports). The ticket also gives reductions on a limited number of tourist attractions and services. You can buy them in main Métro stations, at SNCF Railway stations, in tourist offices, banks and some hotels, at Orly and Roissy airports and at the RATP sales office at 53 bis quai des grands Augustins, 6e, or in the place de la Madeleine, 8e. The *Formule 1* ticket gives one day's unlimited travel for a flat fee on the bus, Métro or RER, (first or second), and on SNCF suburban services (second class). The ticket can cover one, two, three or four zones, or all zones plus the airports. The best value if you are staying for a week is the *Carte Orange*. You need a coupon to go with it. The *Coupon Jaune* runs from Monday to Sunday night, a *Coupon Orange* runs for a calendar month. You can buy it a week before the beginning of each month. You need a passport photo. Tickets are available on the spot (they take about five minutes to process) from Métro stations, some banks and the Tourist Office. For Métro, RER and bus information telephone: RATP 43.46.14.14. For suburban trams telephone: SNCF 45.82.50.50.

Electricity
220V. Two round pins is the most common kind of plug and socket arrangement. An adaptor is needed for American appliances.

Embassies
American Embassy
2 avenue Gabriel, 8e
Tel: 42.96.12.02
British Embassy
Tel: 42.66.91.42
Canadian Embassy
35 avenue Montaigne, 8e
Tel: 47.23.01.01

Emergency
Police–Accidents: Tel: 17
Fire Department: Tel: 18
24-hour emergency treatment:
Blood transfusions Tel: 43.07.47.28
Poison Centre Tel: 42.05.63.29
Samu (accidents) Tel: 45.67.50.50
Serious burns (adults) Tel: Hôpital Cochin 42.34.17.58
Serious burns (children) Tel: Hôpital Trousseau 43.46.13.90
SOS Dentaire (dental emergencies) Tel: 43.37.51.00
(20.00 until midnight)

SOS Médecin (doctor) Tel:
43.37.77.77

Entertainment

For what's going on in English
Tel: 47.20.88.98 or access the
Minitel system *(see
Information).*

You can get a free copy of the
monthly *Paris Selection*
magazine from the Tourist
Office, or buy *Pariscope* or
l'Officiel des Spectacles weekly
(in French) or the rather more
expensive *Passion* magazine (in
English) published by *Time Out*
every two months.

Events

Bastille Day, 14 July, the day that
marked the start of the French
Revolution in 1789, when the
people of Paris stormed the
prison, is always celebrated
with military processions and
fireworks.

For a more detailed listing of
Paris annual events, see pages
93-94.

The Tourist Office publish a
booklet *Saison de Paris* which
lists details of events and major
exhibitions.

Guidebooks

Serious sightseers will find the
green *Michelin* guide to Paris,
or the *Blue Guide to Paris and
Environs* indispensable
companions.

Art lovers interested in galleries
as well as museums will find the
Paris Art Guide useful.

For hotels and restaurants you
will need the slim red *Michelin
Paris* guide or the free guides to
Hotels and Restaurants from the
Paris Tourist Office.

Le Gault Millau is a huge tome
that includes individual write-
ups of over 700 restaurants, as
well as food shops, bars,
nightclubs and hotels.

If you are on a budget, both the
Rough Guide to Paris and
Paupers' Paris by Miles Turner
should save you money during
your stay in Paris.

Helicopter

Should you want a bird's eye
view of Paris contact:
Hélicap Tel: 45.57.75.51
Héli-France Tel: 45.57.53.67
Héli-Promenade Tel: 46.34.16.18

Holidays – Public

New Year's Day
Easter Monday
Labour Day – 1 May
V.E. Day – 8 May
Ascension Day
Whit Monday
Bastille Day – 14 July
Assumption Day – 15 August
All Saints' Day – 1 November
Armistice Day – 11 November
Christmas Day

Hospitals

American Hospital

63 boulevard Victor Hugo,
Neuilly, 5 miles (8km) from the
centre. Tel: 47.47.53.00

British Hospital

48 rue de Villiers, 92 Levallois-
Perret, 5 miles (8km) from the
centre. Tel: 47.58.13.12

Information

The main tourist office is at 127
Champs-Elysées (tel:
47.23.61.72), on the left, at the
top just before the Arc de
Triomphe. It is open every day
from 9:00 A.M. to 8:00 P.M. They
will call around (for a booking
fee) to find a hotel room for you
(cancelled if you do not turn up
within one and a half hours) and
will supply you with brochures,

Excusez-moi, Monsieur l'agent . . .
It pays to address any Parisian
politely, especially a member of the
gendarmerie

free city and Métro maps and
limitless information on the city.
There are also tourist offices at
the main stations (Gare du Nord,
Gare de l'Est, Gare de Lyon,
Gare d'Austerlitz) and at the
Eiffel Tower (from 11:00 A.M. to
6:00 P.M.) from May until the end
of September.
Tourist information (in English)
is available round the clock by
phoning: (1) 47.20.88.98.
Minitel, a computer connected
to the telephone system,
provides information on
practically any service. Use it to
check flight details, book tours,
obtain theatre tickers or even a
Saturday night 'date'. Available
at main post offices. A charge is
made according to access time.

Lost Property
36 rue des Morillons 15e.
(*Métro:* Convention). Visit in
person, as information is not

given over the 'phone. Open
9:00 A.M. to 6:00 P.M.

Money Matters

Banks are open on weekdays
from 9:00 A.M. till noon and 2:00
till 4:00 P.M. (earlier on the day
before a bank holiday). They
are closed on either Saturday or
Monday. You can also change
money at foreign exchange
offices at the airports and main
stations (as well as in stores like
Printemps and Galeries
Lafayette). There is an
automatic exchange machine
(open 24 hours) in the Point-
Show Gallery, Champs-Elysées.
On weekends you can change
money at:
Banco Central, Gare d'Austerlitz
(daily 7:00 A.M. to 9:00 P.M.)
CCF, 117 Champs-Elysées, 8e
(Saturday 8:30 A.M. to 8:00 P.M.)
UBP 154 Champs-Elysées, 8e at
weekends 10:30 A.M. to 6:00 P.M.
CIC Gare de Lyon (daily
6:30 A.M. to 11:00 P.M.)
CIC Georges Pompidou Centre
(noon to 7:00 P.M. daily and from
10:00 A.M. to 7:00 P.M. on
Saturday and Sunday. Closed
Tuesday)
Thomas Cook, Gare du Nord
(daily 6:30 A.M. to 10:00 P.M.,
Monday to Friday)
Thomas Cook, Gare Saint-
Lazare (daily 7:00 A.M. to
9:00 P.M.).

Credit cards

You can use credit cards in
some hotels and restaurants, but
not usually in small shops, or
cafés.
The main numbers for reporting
a loss (24 hrs) are:
American Express 47.77.72.00
Diners' Club 47.62.75.00
Eurocard Mastercard 45.67.84.84

Visa and Carte Bleue 42.77.11.90
You should also report the loss
to the nearest police station and
obtain a written statement from
them to support any subsequent
claim.

Tax

It is a bit of a hassle but you can
get a discount of 13 to 18 per
cent on goods bought for export
if you shop at a store that is
prepared to deal with the
formalities. Ask if they offer *le
détaxe*.
You will probably find that the
minimum purchase is usually
1200F per article.
You have to pay in full and fill in
a form which you then hand into
Customs as you leave with a
stamped addressed envelope.
The tax discount will be sent on
to you. There is a special desk
on the main concourse at Orly
airport and on the third floor in
the departure building at
Charles-de-Gaulle airport to
deal with the paperwork. The
amount of tax varies according
to the type of article bought.
The discount of 18 per cent
applies to perfumes, furs,
jewellery and camera
equipment. You can claim for 13
per cent on other articles.

Opening Times

Museums

National museums close on
Tuesdays (except Versailles
and Musée d'Orsay which are
closed on Monday). Most other
Paris museums are shut on
Mondays and free or half-price
on Sundays. National museums
are free for under 18's and half
price for 18–25-year-olds.
Go early in the morning or be

prepared to wait in line for popular museums like the Louvre, Beaubourg or the Musée d'Orsay.

If you plan to take in several museums it is worth buying a *Carte-Inter-Musées* (see **Tight Budget**).

Shops

Most shops open from 9:00 or 10:00 A.M. to 8:00 P.M. Some shops shut for lunch between noon and 2:00 P.M. and all day on Sunday and Monday. Large department stores open from 9:30 A.M. to 6:30 P.M. and until 8:00 or 10:00 P.M. one or two days a week (usually Wednesday). Food shops open from Monday or Tuesday to Saturday from 7:00 A.M. to 1:30 P.M. and again from 4:00 P.M. until 8:30 P.M. Some are open on Sunday morning until noon.

Pharmacies

Recognised by a green cross. British-American Pharmacy, 1 rue Auber, 9e. English-speaking

The Musée d'Orsay on the Left Bank attracted four million visitors in its first year of opening

staff. Open 8:30 A.M. to 8:00 P.M. Closed Sunday.

Pharmacie Anglaise des Champs-Elysées, 62 Avenue des Champs-Elysées, 8e. Open until 10:30 P.M., closed Sunday.

Pharmacie des Arts, 106 Boulevard Montparnasse, 14e. Open until midnight. 9:00 A.M. to 1:00 P.M. on Sunday.

Pharmacie Dhéry, 84 avenue des Champs-Elysées, 8e. Open all night, 7 days a week.

Pharmacie Opéra, 6 boulevard des Capucines. Open until 12:30 A.M.

Pharmacie Machelon, 5 place Pigalle. Open until 1:00 A.M.

Pharmacie d'Italie, 61 avenue d'Italie. Open until midnight.

Pharmacie Mozart, 14 avenue Mozart. Open until 10:00 P.M. Closed on Sunday.

Places of Worship

There are more than 150 churches and religious buildings in Paris. To find out times and places of services of all denominations contact the Centre d'Information et de Documentation Religieuse, 8 rue Massillon Tel: 46.33.01.01.

Anglican (Episcopalian)

Saint George's Church, 7 rue Auguste-Vacquerie, 16e

The American Cathedral, 23 avenue George V, 8e

Buddhist

Temple Bouddhique, 40 route de Ceinture du Lac Daumesnil, 12e

Catholic

Cathédral of Notre-Dame de Paris, 6 Parvis Notre-Dame, 1er

Sacré-Cœur of Montmartre, 36 rue du Chevalier de la Barre, 18e

Saint Joseph's Church, 50 avenue Hoche, 8e

La Madeleine, place de la Madeleine, 8e

French Reformed Church (Protestant)

Poosy l'Annonciation, 10 rue Cortambert, 16e

Temple de l'Oratoire, 147 rue Saint-Honoré, 1er

Jewish

Synagogue, 17 rue St-Georges, 9e

Lutheran

Eglise des Billettes, 24 rue des Archives, 4e

Eglise Baptiste, 48 rue de Lille, 7e

Moslem

Grand Mosquée, 39 rue Geoffroy-St-Hilaire, 5e

Orthodox

Greek Cathedral of Saint-Etienne, 7 rue Georges Bizet, 16e

Russian Cathedral Sainte-Alexandre, 12 rue Daru, 8e

Police (see **Emergency**)

Police HQ: 7 boulevard du Palais, 4e. Tel: 42.60.33.22

Post Office

Stamps can be bought in post offices and at shops with a 'T' (tabac) sign displayed.

Post Offices (PTT) are open from 8:00 A.M. to 7:00 P.M., Monday to Friday and from 8:00 A.M. to noon on Saturday. The central post office in Paris is at 52 rue du Louvre, 1er (they are open 24 hours a day). They will keep your poste restante letters.

The post office at 71 avenue des Champs-Elysées is also open on Sundays and public holidays. Mailboxes are oblong, stuck

La Madeleine

into walls and a mustard colour. If you are mailing abroad and you get a choice of slots look for one saying *départements étrangers*.

Public Transportation
RATP (buses) 43.46.14.14
SNCF (trains) 24hr information.
Tel: 45.82.50.50

Restaurants
Most restaurants open from noon until 2:30 P.M. for lunch and from 7:00 to 9:30 or 11:00 P.M. for dinner, although cafés and brasseries have longer hours and may stay open until as late as 1:00 A.M. During the day you can get snacks at *salons de thé*. Many restaurants are closed on weekends. You should book a table for the better-known ones. A free guide is available from tourist offices.

Restrooms
Most of the old *pissoirs* have gone, to be replaced by sterile booth-like unisex restrooms. In public places you are expected to tip 2F to the attendant. You may be given toilet paper on your way in. Take toilet paper or tissues with you as many restrooms in cheaper bars and restaurants do not have it.

Senior Citizens
Whatever your nationality you can get a *Carte Vermeil* which allows over-60-year-old women and over-65-year-old men discounts in museums, on public transport and in places of entertainment (up to 50 per cent). Take your passport on arrival to the *Abonnement* office in any of the main railway stations or to the SNCF office which is on the ground floor of the main tourist office at 127 Champs-Elysées, 8e (Métro:

George V). The *Carte* is valid
for a year (from June to May)
and currently costs 65F.
If you have not got the *Carte*,
show your passport whenever
you have to pay an entrance fee.
You may find you still get the
discount.

Students
Reduced prices if you show
your student card.
18–25-year-olds get in half-price
to National Museums.

Swimming
The Piscine Deligny at 25 Quai
Anatole France between the
Pont de la Concorde and the
Solférino pedestrian bridge on

*The 'official' place for
sunbathers is round the piscine
Deligny on the Left Bank, near the
Musée d'Orsay*

the Left Bank near the Musée
d'Orsay is open-air and filled
with clean, recycled Seine
water. The in place for
sunbathing in the summer.
Alternatively there is an outdoor
pool (and an indoor one) at
Molitor, built in 1929 on the
edge of the Bois de Boulogne
(2–8 avenue de la Porte-Molitor,
16e) and an indoor and outdoor
pool in the Butte-aux-Cailles at
5 Verlaine, 13e. Right in the
centre of the city there is an

indoor pool at the Nouveau Forum, the Piscine des Halles, 10 rue de la Rotonde, opposite the church of St-Eustache. The Piscine Keller at 8 rue de l'Ingénieur-Robert- Keller, 15e is popular with serious swimmers.

Telephone

In public places look for a PTT sign. There are often public telephones in bars and brasseries as well as kiosks in the street or at stations. In bars the phone may require a *jeton* which you can buy over the counter or there may be a meter and you settle up after the call.

The French also use magnetic telecards (*télécartes*) which you can buy from post offices, *cafés tabac*, and railway stations.

The French ringing tone is a series of short, regular bleeps. French phone numbers have eight digits. If you have seven add a 4 at the beginning.

To phone anywhere in France from Paris precede 8 digit numbers with 16 (to phone Paris from outside the city precede the number with 161).

Directory Information: (in French) 12

International directory enquiry: 19.33.12 + the country code

To phone the United States dial 19 + 1, the area code (without the initial 0) and then the number. For the United Kingdom dial 19.44 and then the area code (leaving out the initial 0) and then the number.

To reverse the charges (call collect) dial 19.33 and then the country code. Incoming calls can be received at booths with a blue bell sign.

Telegram by phone: (in English) 42.33.21.11. Seven words minimum.

Ticket Agencies

Most agencies charge 20–25 per cent on top of the ticket. Try:
Allo Cheque Théâtre, 33 rue le Peletier, 9e. Tel: 42.46.72.40
Opéra Théâtre, 1 rue Auber, 9e. Tel: 47.42.85.84
The Kiosque Théâtre, place de la Madeleine, or RER Châtelet des Halles sells half-price tickets from 12:45 P.M. until 7:00 P.M. (on the day of the performance) Tuesday to Saturday.
The FNAC bookshops sell tickets for music venues.

Time

Central European Time: US EST + 6 (Summer US EST + 7)

Tipping

Tipping is not necessary in bars and restaurants where service is *compris*, where it is not (*service non compris*) they will add it on for you but the 15 per cent might come as a bit of a shock on top of a fixed price menu. It is customary to leave your small change on the saucer in a bar or café if you have taken your drink at the counter. Tax and service will be added to hotel bills but you should tip the concierge if he has been helpful in any way.

Porters at railway stations have a set price for wheeling luggage (currently 7.50F).
It is also customary to tip usherettes in the cinema as this is their only form of income. You should also give a few francs to the guide in a museum if you have been on a tour.

LANGUAGE

Useful Words and Phrases

The most useful word in the French language is *s'il vous plaît* or please. You will get a lot further using it after every request than if you leave it out. The French may often be rude but they do not like getting a dose of their own medicine. Also useful is a liberal smattering of *excusez-moi* (excuse me) to prefix questions, followed by *monsieur* or *madame*, depending on who you are talking to.

Drinks

beer/draft une bière/pression
coffee — iced/ un café — glacé/
black/with milk noir/au lait
decaffeinated décaféiné
fresh orange juice une orange pressée
hot chocolate chocolat chaud
milk lait
mineral water l'eau minérale
tea/lemon tea un thé/au citron
herb tea infusion, tisane
tonic Schweppes
wine — white/red le vin — blanc/rouge
wine list la carte des vins

Eating Out

cheapest fixed price menu menu conseillé
fixed price menu prix fixe
all included service compris (s.c.) (i.e. do not tip)
a little more encore un peu
butter le beurre
can I have the bill? L'addition, s'il vous plaît?
cheese fromage
closed . . . Monday fermeture . . . lundi
dessert les desserts
first course hors d'œuvre

have you got a table? avez-vous une table de libre?
I would like/we would like je voudrais/on voudrait
. . . to book a table for two . . . une table pour deux
second course entrée
medium rare à point
menu la carte
rare saignant
salt sel
self service libre service (le self)
snacks casse-croûte
all day à toute heure
to eat manger
to drink boire
very rare bleu
well done bien cuit
waiter/waitress monsieur/mademoiselle
what do you recommend? qu'est-ce que vous recommandez?
where are the restrooms? où sont les toilettes?

Money

bank/exchange banque/bureau de change
can I have a receipt? puis-je avoir un reçu?
can I change travellers' cheques here? puis-je changer des chèques de voyage ici?
cashier la caisse
change la monnaie
do you accept credit cards? acceptez-vous des cartes de crédit?
do you have change? pouvez-vous me faire la monnaie?
how much is it, please? c'est combien, s'il vous plaît?
exchange rate cours de change
money argent
travellers' cheques chèques de voyage

Shopping

closed fermeture

discount clothes dégriffés/soldes permanents/reduits
how many/much? combien?
one of those un/une de ceux-là
open ouvert
retail vente au détail
sale soldes
shop le magasin
stamps les timbres'
tax refund la détaxe
that's enough ça suffit
that is too much c'est trop
that is all c'est tout
this one ceci
that one cela
what do I owe you? combien je vous dois?
wholesale vente en gros

TYPES OF SHOP
bakery la boulangerie
butcher la boucherie
cake shop la pâtisserie
candy store la confiserie
cheese shop la fromagerie
dairy la crémerie
delicatessen charcuterie/ traiteur
fish shop la poissonnerie
food shop une alimentation
grocers' une épicerie
hairdresser le coiffeur
pharmacy la pharmacie
post office le bureau de poste
supermarket le supermarché
take-out (grocer) le traiteur

Travelling Around
bridge pont
bus autobus
bus stop arrêt
I am going to je vais à . . .
I need gasoline j'ai besoin d'essence
I need . . . j'ai besoin de . . .
    a ticket to un billet pour
    a book of tickets un carnet
    a one-way ticket un aller simple
    a roundtrip ticket un aller retour

I want to get off je voudrais descendre
information office syndicat d'initiative/office de tourisme
leave me alone laissez-moi tranquille
my car has broken down ma voiture est en panne
oil huile
parking prohibited défense de stationner/stationnement interdit
parking lot un parking
gas station poste d'essence
gasoline essence
platform quai
plane avion
please direct me to . . . pour aller à . . . s'il vous plaît?
railway station la gare
the road for la route pour
ticket office vente de billets
to cross the road traverser la rue
traffic lights les feux
tires les pneus
subway Métro

Directions
after après
behind derrière
before avant
here ici
in front of devant
left à gauche
near près
opposite en face de
right à droite
straight on tout droit
there là
where? où?
where is? où est?
what time does it arrive/leave /part? il arrive à quelle heure?
where are we on this map? où sommes-nous sur le plan?
where can I find a taxi? où puis-je trouver un taxi?
where is the station? où est la gare?

LANGUAGE

Vocabulary

yes oui
no non
please s'il vous plaît
thank you merci
bad mauvais
big grand
cold froid
condoms preservatifs
day un jour
far loin
goodbye au revoir
good evening bonsoir
good morning bonjour
good night bonne nuit
good bon
hot chaud
later plus tard
month un mois
now maintenant
small petit
today aujourd'hui
under sous
week une semaine
when? quand?
why? pourquoi?
with avec
without sans
yesterday hier

Phrases

at what time? à quelle heure?
call an ambulance appelez une
    ambulance s'il vous plaît
could you speak more slowly?
    pouvez-vous parler plus
    lentement, s'il vous plaît?
do you speak English? parlez-vous
    anglais?
help! au secours!
how much is this? combien?
I do not understand je ne
    comprends pas
I need a doctor je voudrais voir un
    docteur
I want je voudrais
Is there someone here who
    speaks English? Y a-t-il quelqu'un
    qui parle anglais ici?

I'm sorry pardon
please could you write it down?
    pouvez-vous me l'écrire?
thank you very much merci
    beaucoup
where is the nearest police
    station? où est le post de
    police le plus proche?

Numbers

one un
two deux
three trois
four quatre
five cinq
six six
seven sept
eight huit
nine neuf
ten dix
first premier (-ière)
second seconde (deuxième)
third troisième
fourth quatrième
fifth cinqième

Days of the Week

Monday lundi
Tuesday mardi
Wednesday mercredi
Thursday jeudi
Friday vendredi
Saturday samedi
Sunday dimanche
festivals/holidays fêtes/jours fériés

Months of the Year

January janvier
February février
March mars
April avril
May mai
June juin
July juillet
August aôut
September septembre
October octobre
November novembre
December décembre
Christmas Noël
Easter Pâques